ABOUT THE AUTHORS

Dr Richard Keegan is a senior specialist at Enterprise Ireland, in the areas of World Class Business and Benchmarking. He has written extensively in the area of benchmarking and World Class Manufacturing/Business, and is the author of *World Class Manufacturing ... in an Irish Context* (with John J Lynch), *An Introduction to World Class Manufacturing*, and *Benchmarking Facts* (all published by Oak Tree Press). He is a staff member at University of Dublin, Trinity College.

Eddie O'Kelly is the first Chairperson of EirGrid plc, the company that is being set up to become the Transmission System Operator in Ireland, and is Emeritus Professor of Industrial Engineering, National University of Ireland, Galway. With qualifications in the fields of electrical, mechanical, industrial and management engineering, he was previously a Board member and Deputy Chairman of the Electricity Supply Board (ESB) and a Director of ESB International (ESBI), Director of a number of private companies and, until 1998, acted as Chairperson of the FÁS Retail Advisory Committee. He has wide experience of working with State bodies and private companies as a consultant.

APPLIED BENCHMARKING FOR COMPETITIVENESS

A Guide for SME Owner/Managers

Richard Keegan
Eddie O'Kelly

www.oaktreepress.com

OAK TREE PRESS
19 Rutland Street, Cork, Ireland
http://www.oaktreepress.com

© 2004 Richard Keegan and Eddie O'Kelly

A catalogue record of this book is
available from the British Library.

ISBN 1-86076-271-9

Printed in Ireland by ColourBooks.

CONTENTS

FIGURES

CASE STUDIES

DEDICATIONS

To Geraldine, Aoife and Maeve, thank you for your love, support and laughter – all essential to the completion of this project.

Richard

In grateful appreciation to Jane + 6 for sharpening my understanding of "Best in Class".

EOK

THANKS

With special thanks to all the companies and colleagues who have helped to make this book a reality. Particular thanks to Mike and Sheila for covering so well, your help and support is greatly appreciated.

Thanks to Enterprise Ireland for supporting this work.

FOREWORD

Europe is getting bigger and the world is getting smaller. Irish companies today are as likely to be competing for business with companies in Birmingham, Berlin or Bejing as they are with those in Ballyfermot, Galway or Limerick. The level of competition is rising all the time, with companies no longer able to rely on their island status or their physical closeness to customers. But just what is the level of competition and how can companies act to become more competitive?

Major corporations on both sides of the Atlantic have been tackling these problems for a number of years. With the advent of the Global Economy, it has become very important for successful companies to be able to:

- Identify what the true level of competition is
- What key priorities lead to superior performance
- Manage action programmes to improve effectiveness, efficiency and, ultimately, competitiveness.

The multi-nationals have worked with, and developed responses in, the areas of benchmarking and best practice under the names of Just In Time, Total Quality Management, Lean Production, Value Analysis and Value Engineering, Quality Function Deployment, Six Sigma and a host of others. In Ireland, we have known these best practice techniques as World Class techniques – a rose by any other name!

What works for the multi-nationals with all their resources, money, and structures certainly will not work for typical small and medium-sized companies, at least not without being adapted for their needs and resources. This book presents the proven results of such an adaptation process, where Irish small and medium-sized companies have used a combination of benchmarking and world class techniques to improve their businesses' profitability, their capabilities and their performance – using what can be called "Applied Benchmarking for Competitiveness – the ABC of company development".

IS THERE A PROBLEM?

It seems strange to say that there *is* a problem with Irish companies. Surely, given the era of the Celtic Tiger, we must be one of the most competitive countries in the world? Like the curate's egg, the answer to this question is "in places"! Yes, at a national level, we do rank among the top EU countries in terms of productivity, a key element of competitiveness. Ireland ranks near or at the top of the European productivity ladder for companies employing over 50 people but, for companies employing less than 50 people, we are at or near the bottom of the European productivity ladder, we rank 15th out of 17 in Europe, including Norway and Switzerland. It is clear that there is definitely a problem.

This problem is quite serious for a number of reasons:

- We have a lot of SMEs – 98% of Irish companies employ less than 50 people
- Our SMEs supply our larger companies – if our SMEs are not efficient, then our larger companies cannot be.
- SMEs provide the backbone of our country, with most small and medium-sized companies doing business with a 50km radius.

What makes the difference between the big and small/medium companies? It would be easy to say that the big companies have more money, resources and staff to improve their performance. They usually have. There are obvious differences, usually in terms of capital invested, product design and innovation, systems employed and general resources available to the big companies to tackle problems as they arise. But there are also obvious similarities – many rely on Irish staff to use their mental capacity to solve problems, and to improve operational performance. This key factor, the mental capacity of our people to solve problems and improve performance, is the key to sustained competitiveness. We need to maximise the potential of our people to deliver improved productivity using proven tools and techniques, if we are to rise from the position of 15th in European productivity.

The opportunity to develop our competitiveness is available to us now. At the individual company level, we cannot affect the issues of taxation, education and infrastructure. We can hope to influence developments through representation and lobbying, of course, but the decision-making process is out of our hands.

Enterprise Ireland's experience with Benchmarking and Best Practice, working with Irish companies, shows that this approach works and leads to improved competitiveness. Case studies are presented throughout this book, outlining the results achieved by Irish companies using the tools. The challenge is for more businesses to adopt these tools and make their own improvements.

We *can* affect how we perform in our own businesses. We *can* change how we do things, we *can* change the things we have control over. This book will focus on just these things, on practical tools and techniques that you can learn about and adapt and adopt for your own company's circumstances, needs and resources. The basics of Applied Benchmarking for Competitiveness – the ABC of company development – will be explained in this book.

Dr Brendan Finucane
Director Technology
Enterprise Ireland

1: APPLIED BENCHMARKING FOR COMPETITIVENESS

Applied Benchmarking for Competitiveness (ABC) is a simple approach to help companies to diagnose objectively, efficiently and effectively their current situation and to take steps to improve performance. ABC combines the basics of benchmarking and World Class Business (WCB) techniques in a proven, effective form for small and medium-sized companies. By taking a core of benchmarking and WCB techniques, companies can quickly achieve significant performance improvements.

Using a medical analogy, benchmarking can be seen as the diagnosis and the world class business techniques as the medicine. Benchmarking acts as the diagnosis, an objective look at your business with a view to identifying issues and areas requiring attention and improvement, as well as identifying areas where you may exhibit performance superior to others in your sector.

Taking this medical analogy further, imagine you went to the doctor and were told that, yes, you were unwell, were asked for payment and shown the door. You would have known already that you were unwell before the visit, that's why you went to the doctor in the first place; now you are still unwell and your wallet is also lighter.

If a company simply benchmarks itself and then takes no action for improvement, it will have made the diagnosis but not taken the medicine. The basic World Class tools and techniques provide the medicine, actions that can be taken to help to solve problems and improve performance.

Developing the medical analogy a stage further again, if your doctor told you the medicine you needed to take was 1gm of sodium met-bisulphate, 0.02 gm of carbon tetrachloride and 0.001gm of xylene in a calcium base, you would be flummoxed. The same situation exists for a business. It is not enough to know which tools are needed to be used, it is often necessary to know when given tools are appropriate, and to understand the sequence of use. Therefore, this book explains:

- What is benchmarking
- What are the World Class Business tools and techniques
- How can they be used by small and medium-sized businesses to improve their performance.

By doing this, the book attempts to address some of the key issues facing business today:

- Matching the improvement process to the needs and resources of SMEs
- Identifying an effective and efficient transfer mechanism, to help build internal capability in SMEs
- Developing an approach to best practice transfer that could form the basis for a semi-standardised approach for SME development.

The tools and techniques are presented at three levels. We suggest that companies master the tools and techniques at Level 1 before moving on to Levels 2 and 3. By learning and using the basic tools of Level 1, a company will build its staff's capability and prepare itself for the more demanding tools and techniques of Levels 2 and 3.

BUSINESSES ARE COMPLEX

A business is made up of many parts, often dependent on each other. One of the most frequently encountered problems in a business is that the individual elements or departments are often unaware of how they affect or impact on each other. Often a business run by engineers believes that the acquisition of the latest technology will give them a lead in the market. A business run by marketing people often believes that a full focus on marketing will bring them success. And a business run by an accountant believes that they would be successful, if only the marketing and engineering people would stop spending the money!

The truth of the matter is that a successful business needs awareness and understanding, ability and focused effort in all areas of the business. One area may be its key strength but, to perform well in highly competitive markets, businesses need not only key strengths but also need to minimise weaknesses throughout the business.

When looking at a business, it is important to be aware of this complexity, to understand what is actually happening in the business, ABC helps you to do just this, by dealing with the key elements of a successful business: Strategies; Sales & Marketing; Operations; Innovation; People; and Finance.

For a company to be successful, it must understand the interaction of these key elements within its business. If the business has no strategic goal, or has no objective for the future, it can be difficult to motivate people towards success. Unless it can sell its products to markets large enough to sustain the business, then the future will be bleak. Operations need to be able to source parts, to build products and to deliver them on time, at a cost and to a quality standard suited to the marketplace. The design group need to be able to develop innovative products to meet, and exceed, market desire. The people within a business *are* the business. Without their skill, effort and flair, a business has no chance of success. And finance, to support the business and to capture a return from the efforts of all, is essential for success.

A successful business understands and develops the interactions between these key elements. By doing this, the business and its people will move up the spiral of performance.

WHAT IS BENCHMARKING?

Benchmarking is a way of helping organisations to compare themselves against others, in order to learn from others. It provides a proven mechanism to help identify and prioritise areas for improvement within a business in an objective manner, as well as providing a simple way to measure progress over time. Benchmark results recorded today will facilitate measuring what progress has been made in a year's time.

In Europe, benchmarking is defined as:

> "… a continuous, systematic process for comparing performances of organisations, functions or processes against the 'best in the world', aiming not only to match those performance levels, but to exceed them."
> **DG Enterprise, European Commission**

Benchmarking is used by large and multi-national companies to compare themselves against others and to help them in their improvement processes. For small and medium-sized companies, the issue is not usually about adopting "best in the world" standards but more often about using current good practice throughout the business.

Benchmarking allows a business to identify objectively key business processes and the issues within them. It helps to identify and eliminate waste, to find ways, proven by others, to improve performance across the key areas of the business and so increase profitability and market share. A key strength of the benchmarking approach is that it helps managers to make decisions based on facts, rather than on opinion or intuition. Many management decisions are taken with incomplete data. Using benchmarking, managers can know the performance levels of their peers and competitors and what practices they use to achieve these performance levels.

The benchmarking definition refers to benchmarking as being a continuous, systematic process. Why continuous? What is the point of benchmarking a business or organisation today and never again? Unless a business continues to monitor progress over time, all it will achieve by benchmarking once is a snapshot of how the business compares with others, at that time. By using benchmarking continuously, it can monitor progress or maybe see none and use this as a stimulus to staff to look for other means of improvement or superior effort.

A small number of key performance indicators (KPIs), can be included in regular management reporting mechanisms. Examples of these KPIs could be daily, weekly or monthly sales, on-time deliveries, monthly profitability, quality complaints or other measures specific to the business. The regular tracking and management of the business to these measures between benchmarking exercises can help focus people's minds on achieving business and organisational goals.

Why a systematic process? One of the problems with benchmarking is ensuring that like-with-like comparisons are made. Just how can a small pottery in the extreme south-west of Ireland compare itself with a business operating in Berlin? By using a systematic approach, the differences and similarities between business and organisations can be accommodated and normalised. The use of a systematic benchmarking approach ensures comparability between companies, organisations, regions and countries, as well as ensuring repeatability over time. If the same approach is followed, using the same system, ensuring the quality and accuracy of data, then it is possible to compare and learn from companies across the world, as shown by the two leading small and medium-sized company benchmarking tools: Microscope and Benchmark Index.

The benchmarking process can help management to identify and prioritise areas requiring change and improvement, as well as providing a means of monitoring and measuring progress over time. Modern benchmarking tools have been developed to present results graphically, helping management to visualise relative performance strengths and weaknesses and to prioritise improvement activities.

WHAT GETS MEASURED, IMPROVES

Experience with small and medium-sized businesses shows that they often do not measure performance in many areas. One of the dangers with measurement is ensuring the right things are measured. It is important to know what customers find important and use this as a key performance measure within the operation.

The basis of business and competition has changed dramatically over the past 10 to 15 years. While managers of many Western companies believed that a company competed on price or quality alone, the Japanese started to compete in a different way. They provided not only low-cost but also high-quality and superior features. This led the European and American car companies to the point of crisis in the early 1980s. Since then the "mass production" approach pioneered by Henry Ford has given way to the "mass customisation" of today's best manufacturers.

To compete effectively in today's markets, companies need to be competitive simultaneously on price, delivery, quality, responsiveness, flexibility, and innovation. This is a difficult and complex set of factors and is obviously dependent on a complete business response rather than a single department. Given this shift in the field of competition, European business can no longer rely on simple, traditional measures, often used singly.

Seven key characteristics of appropriate measures for this new competitive environment have been identified (Maskell). Factors should:

- Be directly related to the strategy
- Include non-financial, as well as financial
- Vary between locations, dependent on market
- Change over time
- Be simple and easy-to-use and understand
- Provide fast feedback to operators and managers

- Teach rather than monitor.

Looking at these characteristics, it is clear that any measures adopted by a small to medium-sized company need to be chosen carefully. The lack of available time means that, unless both managers and staff can see how the measure is relevant, they are unlikely to use it. This is a centrally important point: unless a measure is used, it is worthless. The information being captured needs to be analysed and used to help improve the process. There is no point in knowing that something is not good within your operation, unless you do something to fix the problem. The World Class techniques outlined in this book can be adapted to improve your operations.

WHY USE BENCHMARKING?

Benchmarking is objective. It is often difficult for people to be objective about things they are closely involved with. How can people be expected to be objective about a business where they spend seven to 10 hours every working day? Benchmarking enables people to compare their business to other companies in their sector, of similar size. It allows them to understand what others are doing to get their levels of performance and can help them identify key issues the company faces if it is to improve performance.

Benchmarking also provides the opportunity to compare a business against international levels of practice and performance. By accessing international benchmarking tools, small and medium-sized companies can gain valuable insights into how their international competitors work. Given the increasing levels of competition from companies located overseas, this is very important. It provides a means of identifying real competitiveness levels and also of learning how to achieve them.

Benchmarking also provides a logical way to help business prioritise their improvement actions. Few, if any, small and medium-sized companies have spare resources, whether of time or money, to be able to tackle all their issues at one time. Also, many managers are faced with identifying issues in areas of the business they may not be fully comfortable with. Often, managers in small and medium-sized companies wear more than one "hat", and can lack the training or experience to identify issues outside their primary area. By using a benchmarking approach that addresses the key areas of a business, they can be helped to identify true issues and to construct actions to address them, in a prioritised way.

A LEARNING OPPORTUNITY

To be a success, it is important to learn with, and from, others. Learning by example, by watching others, is one of the most basic forms of learning. From the days of our early childhood, we learned from watching and listening to others. We learned to walk, speak and ride a bicycle from others. This process of learning from others can often help us achieve difficult and demanding goals.

In the business world, benchmarking provides the opportunity to observe, to learn from others with a view to adapting for our own circumstances. A key point to remember in the business context is that, as children, we often fell down or failed at our early attempts to master a new technique. In business, we may need to use the same perseverance to ensure long-term success.

> If a thing is worth doing, it's worth doing badly at first.
> **Anon.**

A clear link has been found between the practices that a business or organisation uses and the level of performance it achieves. The best companies and organisations in the world today, truly World Class organisations, exhibit high levels of both practice use and performance achieved. These same organisations are often front-runners in adopting and developing current best practice. They are, in effect, learning organisations: learning from their own internal experiences, as well as from the shared experience of others. These leading organisations use benchmarking to check their positions relative to others in their own sector, region, country or on a world-wide basis. Even more importantly, they take every opportunity to learn from, and with, other leading organisations, organisations that themselves are pushing the boundaries of efficiency and effectiveness. A common feature of many of these organisations, both commercial, industrial and public sector, is the belief and realisation that, although they may currently hold leading positions within their sphere of operations, they need to constantly improve their performance across their operations if they are to secure their positions into the future. They recognise the need to improve constantly, to follow the "Continuous Improvement" or "Kaizen" route, using the tools of

World Class Business to improve their performance, across all elements of their business.

The story is told of the Ford Motor Company when they developed a close relationship with Mazda of Japan. Ford had always been proud of its ability in terms of purchasing and materials acquisition and was regarded, by other Western companies, as the leader in these areas. When Ford staff got close to Mazda, they were astounded to see that Mazda used 80% fewer staff per car to acquire parts and components. They were five times more efficient than Ford! Clearly, this revelation led to some serious soul-searching, analysis and improvement within Ford. This practical benchmark exercise led to significant savings for Ford, and a new way of operating. Change and development, and improving operational performance are directly linked to learning. We must learn and develop, if we are to improve. We need to learn new things, concepts and techniques, if we are to identify areas for improvement and implement change, or if we are to secure superior performance.

But, change can be difficult. If we are comfortable in our ways of operating, if our company or organisation is meeting its goals, why should we change? We must change, develop and improve, if we are to ensure survival and growth into the future. When a company or an organisation starts to introduce change, it often runs into resistance. One of the most common types of resistance is the "not invented here" syndrome.

People can often feel that if an idea or concept did not originate in their organisation, then it is worthless. The counter argument is why do we individually have to re-invent the wheel? If another organisation has already found a better solution to a problem, why should we refuse to accept it? If we take the opportunity to compare our solution with a better one from another source, we may well be able to improve even on it. Benchmarking provides the opportunity and the process to learn with, and from, others.

A key factor in benchmarking is that it provides the opportunity for people at all levels in an organisation to learn and develop. Our European workforce is generally well-educated. We should remember that the mass production approach developed by Ford and General Motors was designed to manage a workforce that frequently did not speak a common language and was generally poorly educated. Surely the time has come to benefit from the high level of education and intelligence of our workforces? By adopting current best practice in business, by using benchmarking to learn about these practices and how they can relate to our own operations, by using quality management techniques to implement the changes identified, we can achieve significant improvements in our operational performance. We can measure these improvements with our traditional measurements such as profit and manage with the new measures such as lead-time and customer responsiveness. Europe has the opportunity to learn from others, both within the Community and outside, and to avoid having to make the mistakes others have had to go through in our efforts to improve competitiveness.

2: The Diagnosis: Qualitative & Quantitative Benchmarking

Benchmarking is not a new concept. In our daily lives, we constantly deal with benchmarks: which is the best football team, which is the fastest car or the one with the best fuel consumption? Our interaction with benchmarking started when we were very young. Were we above or below average height or weight, were our school results keeping up to standard? Most of these benchmarks were based on numbers, known as quantitative benchmarks.

Ratio benchmarking is based on numbers. However, the numbers alone do not give the full picture and are often not enough to help people understand what and how they can do to improve their performance. Consider a football example in **Figure 1**, to see how the numbers do not always tell the full picture – in particular, how to focus improvement efforts.

FIGURE 1: DETERMINING THE TRUE SCORE

	Premier Division	P	F	A	Pts
1	Manchester United	15	36	12	31
2	Blackburn Rovers	15	27	13	30
3	Arsenal	15	30	17	27
...	...				
19	Barnsley	15	12	40	13
20	Everton	15	16	23	12

Looking at the top teams, one might assume that scoring goals is the key to leading the league table, to being a better team. But then why is

Arsenal not ahead of Blackburn? Or one could say that not having goals scored against one's team is best, but then why is Everton not ahead of Barnsley? It is clear the numbers alone do not give a full picture of where a club, or for that matter an organisation, should focus to improve.

The numbers can only tell *what* has been achieved, not *how* it was achieved. It is not enough to know that your competitors are more profitable than you are, you also need to know how they manage to achieve this. Qualitative benchmarking, looking at the practices that organisations employ, helps to answer these questions.

Researchers have studied what leading organisations do, how they manage and organise their people, their systems and their assets. One of these studies (Voss *et al.*) found a positive link between the practices that companies employ and the level of performance they achieve. In simple terms, do the right thing and you will get the benefit!

The combination of qualitative and quantitative benchmarking – looking at the numbers *and* how they are achieved – is an ideal approach to start your improvement activities. Consider a school report in **Figure 2**, which shows a combination of numbers/quantitative measures and process insights/qualitative measures.

FIGURE 2: IDENTIFYING WHERE IMPROVEMENTS SHOULD BE MADE

School Report	
Maths	75%
English	68%
Irish	80%
Comment: Richard could focus on his English, particularly his grammar.	

The school report provides numbers but also some insights into where improvements can, and should, be made. Understanding how the quantitative and qualitative elements of benchmarking interact is critical to maximising the benefits to be obtained from a benchmarking exercise.

In a business context, we are also quite familiar with benchmarks: Stock Exchange ratings, financial reports and internal management accounts are well-known and widely-used. The studies performed by Frederick Taylor on the scientific methods of work organisation are early examples of benchmarking being applied in industry. Much of the advancements made in mass production were related to this work. Ford and General Motors, Renault and Fiat developed the mass production system based on a simplification of processes, working with Taylor's methods. But, in the early stages of the 21st century, we need to look again at the manufacturing systems and concepts that we have grown up with. We must remember that the mass production system was designed to make products effectively and efficiently, with limited variety. The early innovators in mass production were trying to manage a business operating in different competitive circumstances from those of today. The terms of competition in the market place have changed. Today's European managers need to address these changed circumstances, if we are to compete effectively on the world market.

Benchmarking is much more than simply copying competitors' best practices. Dr Deming, a leading American statistician who developed many of today's leading quality tools and approaches, wrote:

> "To copy is too risky, because you don't understand why you are doing it. To ADAPT, and not adopt, is the way".

The Japanese have used these concepts of early benchmarking to great effect over the past 40 years. In the late 1950s and early 1960s, the Japanese were considered to be the masters of copying. However, they were using benchmarking tools to develop their products and processes more efficiently in terms of time and money than their Western competitors. Operating under a specific set of conditions, they adapted their responses accordingly. For example, they identified logistics as a key problem. So, they identified what was regarded as the most effective logistics operations of their time, adapted the supply methods used by the big American supermarket distribution chains, and developed them to create the "Just-in-Time" system.

LEVELS OF BENCHMARKING

As one learns about benchmarking and how it can be used to help improve competitiveness, it is useful to understand how it has evolved over the years.

The evolution of benchmarking can be presented as a series of five steps:

1. **Analysis of competing goods (reverse engineering):** During this first phase, benchmarking concentrated on comparison of characteristics, functionalities and performance of competing products. Initially, this was only at a technical level, but was later expanded to include competitive evaluation of products from a market perspective.

2. **Competitive benchmarking:** First developed by Rank Xerox when starting to analyse its own manufacturing costs (they found these were as high as its competitors' sale prices!). Now the emphasis is on process efficiency, not just product comparisons.

3. **Process benchmarking:** During the 1980s, managers started to realise that they also could learn with organisations from other sectors (benchmarking out of the box). The amount of information and knowledge available amongst non-competing companies was found often to be higher than between competitors.

4. **Strategic benchmarking:** A systematic process to evaluate alternative scenarios, to implement strategies and improve performance through the understanding and adaptation of successful strategies by the partners (competitors or not). It differs from process benchmarking because its scope is larger and deeper.

5. **Global benchmarking:** The next generation concept, that it includes and analyses cultural differences between companies at world-wide level. It takes also into account the conditions (legal, administrative, education, social, environment) that affect the localisation of companies.

Decisive factors for the spread of benchmarking also were the quality award models of the American Malcolm Baldrige National Quality Award (1988) and the European Quality Award (1992). In the quality models, comparisons with competitors and/or best practices are repeatedly requested.

BENCHMARKING AS PART OF THE QUALITY MOVEMENT

Business is under constant pressure to improve, to perform at a higher level. This is as true for service industries as it is for manufacturers or public enterprises. Benchmarking is part of the Quality Management concept and has its roots in industry. Its influence has spread over the past 10 years. Increasingly, organisations like Government agencies, hospitals and schools are discovering the benefit of quality management concepts for their areas of operation. Benchmarking, especially, comparing practices from different areas, is helpful and can often lead to considerable improvements.

As for total quality management, top management support is an essential prerequisite for benchmarking. Without honest and open support of the efforts towards improvement from the top management, no benchmarking project can attain the desired results. In the area of communication, top management can, and must, give the team decisive support. In addition, top management must be prepared to accept less than flattering insights into their own performance capability and to provide the necessary framework conditions for change.

The concept behind quality management tools is about making products or providing services

"Quicker, Better and Cheaper ... Together".

Each of these words covers a wide range of tools and techniques that can range from the very simple to the very complicated. It is fundamentally important to understand that a company or organisation must come to its own understanding of any proposed concept. It needs to take ownership of the concept and modify and apply those elements that are appropriate for it at the particular time. Companies often start at a low level on specific tools, but became more demanding of them as their abilities to use them improve and their understanding of their power develops. The basic requirement to service customer's needs quicker, better or cheaper is common to all organisations, commercial or state. Benchmarking may have its roots in industry but, today, it is being applied by all types of organisations and businesses to help their improvement processes.

Although most current benchmarking practitioners are companies or organisations employing over 1,000 people, benchmarking can, and should, also be applied to small and medium-sized enterprises. SMEs can use benchmarking because current best practice in benchmarking focuses on processes – when comparing processes, it is of little difference whether an organisation has 100 or 10,000 employees.

TYPES OF BENCHMARKING

There are many different ways to define benchmarking. We have already talked about competitive analysis, strategic and sectoral benchmarking. Let's now look at the types of benchmarking a business might get involved with – **Figure 3**.

FIGURE 3: TYPES OF BENCHMARKING

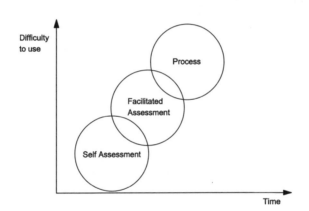

The general types of benchmarking, ranked in terms of ease of use are:

1. Self Assessment
2. Faciliatated Assessment
3. Process.

Each of these tools can be useful and helpful to a business. It is suggested that Self Assessment is very appropriate for companies at Level 1, starting out on the improvement process. Facilitated Assessment benchmarking is helpful to businesses at Level 2, when they have some experience in improving their operations. These businesses can, and do, benefit from the input of an objective viewpoint provided by an outside facilitator. Process benchmarking is often demanding of people, money and commitment and is therefore best suited to businesses operating at Level 3, when they are truly dedicated to improving performance and competing on the open global market. Further information on each type of benchmarking is presented in later sections of this book.

3: THE MEDICINE: A WORLD CLASS BUSINESS TOOLKIT

The medicine is what companies can do to have a positive impact on their performance. When the World Class concept was introduced to Ireland in the mid-1990s, its focus was on manufacturing industry. People thought the ideas and concepts of world class were suited to, and only suitable for, the shop floor. Since then, it has become clear that World Class techniques are equally applicable in a service organisation, a commercial operation or a manufacturing plant.

Irish companies have used the World Class Business approach to help them increase sales, reduce purchasing costs, improve terms of supply, simplify and remove costs from administration, improve product development process, reduce capital requirement, manage outsourced suppliers as well as in the more traditional areas of production and supply chain-logistics.

Irish companies currently using World Class Business approaches span such sectors as advertising, pottery, engineering, food, electronics, printing, furniture, and joinery, medical devices and pharmaceuticals. They range in size from five people to 200, spread across the country. The usefulness of the World Class Business approach is not limited in itself, only by the vision of those using it.

THE BASICS OF WORLD CLASS BUSINESS

World Class Business (WCB) is a response, based on the need for small and medium companies to perform at the highest level to meet the needs of demanding customers in the face of increasingly aggressive international competition. The WCB approach focuses on providing management and staff of small and medium-sized companies with the tools to help them see and understand their business issues and then to implement responses to address these.

The basic concept can be described as the thrust to make products or provide services: "**Quicker, Better, Cheaper .... Together**". These four words capture the essence of WCB.

Why **Quicker**? How many companies have the luxury of providing their service or delivering their product "whenever they are ready with it"? The reality of today's marketplace, with ever shorter lead-times and fierce competition for business, dictates that time is a key factor in a successful business.

Why **Better**? How many customers are prepared to accept quality standards that were acceptable 10 or 20 years ago? No longer is it acceptable to deliver a poor quality service or a bad product. The understanding of quality, as it applies to services and products, is centrally important if operations are to improve.

Why **Cheaper**? Customers and consumers are unlikely to pay more for a product or service than they need to. The pressure of competition has meant that prices for many services and goods have remained at, or around, the same level for many years, when adjusted for inflation, which itself has been historically low. To compete, to stay in business, a focus on costs is needed.

And finally, why **Together?** Experience has shown that groups of people working together can be more effective than a single individual. In the business context, most businesses employ more than one person. For the business to be successful, it is obvious that the different skills, abilities and energies of everybody involved in it need to be harnessed in an effective and efficient way. Anything less is wasting a very precious and costly asset.

These are the basics of World Class Business: **Quicker, Better, Cheaper ... Together**.

But *how* do you do it? The next sections of this chapter will present the tools and techniques that have been developed—and proven – in Irish small and medium-sized companies, to help the owners and staff to use and implement WCB.

THE WORLD CLASS HOUSE

The World Class House was developed to illustrate how the elements of WCB work together (**Figure 4**).

FIGURE 4: WORLD CLASS HOUSE

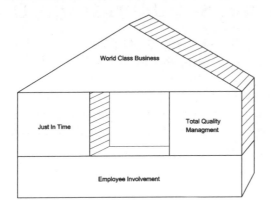

The objective is to build World Class Businesses – that can operate successfully on the world stage, which can compete with the best in the business, profitably. The road to being, and remaining, world class is difficult and demanding. World Class companies will always be looking for their next challenge, the next stretch target for them to achieve.

The foundation for this activity is the people within an organisation or business. Employee involvement presents tools and techniques to help businesses and organisations harness the strengths and abilities of their workforces to achieve a common goal.

To help these businesses reach their targets, Just-in-Time and Total Quality Management are used. Just-in-Time tools help businesses wage a war on waste, across all elements of a business. Although these techniques came from manufacturing, they have been developed and adjusted for the general needs of business. Total Quality Management provides simple tools to help identify and monitor performance. The tools work as effectively in a sales, administration or purchasing environment as they do on the shop floor.

The rest of this chapter presents the tools and techniques of WCB, using case studies based on companies that have used specific tools, in order to describe real life examples of their use.

Although each of the companies in the case studies are shown using only one tool, they have used many of the WCB techniques presented in this book right across their operations, choosing tools as appropriate to their needs. The WCB toolkit is just that, a toolkit, from which each company or organisation can select the appropriate tools for their needs.

LOOK, SEE, UNDERSTAND, DO

The tools and techniques of World Class Business are designed to help a business and its people to: **Look, See, Understand, Do**.

Much of people's time in business is spent handling the "day job", doing what needs to be done. WCB techniques ask the question "What are we trying to achieve here?" and then help the questioner to see what is actually being done – the difference between the question and the answer is the gap that needs to be bridged.

It is not enough to improve things once. Innovation and change needs to be seen as a continuous effort. The challenge is to move a business operation up the Spiral of Performance (see **Figure 5**), looking, seeing and understanding processes before acting to improve them – time after time. As an organisation moves up the spiral, it builds the capability to address ever more important and demanding issues and challenges. It moves to be truly World Class and able to compete on the highest fields.

FIGURE 5: SPIRAL OF PERFORMANCE

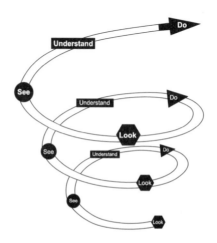

THE BASIC TOOLBOX

The fundamental tools, which seem to be applicable in all businesses (the hammer, screwdriver and pliers, as it were), and which should be in every business' toolbox are:

- Physical Flow
- Process Flow
- Check Sheets
- Run Charts
- Teams.

Physical Flow

One of the simplest tools to use, the physical flow diagram is very helpful in letting one see the "wood for the trees", in seeing the reality of an operation.

The technique maps the movement of work through an operation, whether it is paperwork through the administration area or products through the manufacturing area.

Quite often, processes contain steps that managers are unaware of, steps that have developed over time and become part of how staff do things. By mapping the physical movement through the operation, one can often find waste.

Process Flow

Process flow mapping provides a word picture of the processes used.

The technique has two basic elements:

- Process mapping of the *theoretical* or "best" process
- Process mapping of the *actual* process.

Clearly, the difference between the two is a target for improvement.

Check Sheets

A check sheet is a simple quality tool that lets managers and staff capture real data from operations in an effective and efficient way. The tool is very powerful and easy-to-use.

A list is made of things that happen and, each time one of the items on the list occurs, a tick is placed against that item on the list. By looking at the number of ticks against each item, it is very easy to determine which items occur most often – and, therefore, which should be given priority in any attempt to effect improvements.

Run Charts

The run chart represents performance over time and provides a very quick and easy way of understanding performance.

The tool can be used as effectively to record sales as production output or quality problems.

Teams

Teams are the foundation of a successful World Class Business initiative. The old saying "you pay for the hands, but the minds come free" is very true. The challenge for many businesses is how to harness those minds. The creating and building of a team working environment can be difficult but, when it is achieved, the results can be amazing.

HOW TO USE THIS BOOK

These core tools will be described now in some detail. They provide a very powerful toolkit to start a World Class Business initiative.

This book is structured to meet the needs of businesses that want to improve their performance. Tools and techniques that have been proven to work in Irish companies are presented at three levels:

- **Level 1:** Basic tools, proven to be both easy-to-use and effective in operation, which provide a foundation for all businesses, managers and employees, irrespective of sector or size of operation.

- **Level 2:** Intermediate tools, suited to businesses that are interested in improving their performance, probably those interested in selling overseas, willing to face the challenge of open competition. These tools and techniques will help managers and staff to work together in identifying areas for improvement. They will help also to focus attention on future possibilities for superior performance.

- **Level 3:** Advanced tools, identified as being those suited to the needs of businesses that need to perform at the highest international level. These tools are demanding of a business but are equally rewarding.

At each level, the appropriate type of benchmarking is presented and explained:

- At Level 1, basic Self Assessment is introduced – metrics for performance, based on Island of Ireland statistics, are available at www.irishbenchmarkingforum.com.
- At Level 2, Facilitated Self Assessment is introduced, along with some international insights into the leading benchmarking tools of Microscope (www.comparisoninternational.com) and BenchmarkIndex (www.benchmarkindex.com).
- Level 3 uses Process Benchmarking.

The materials are presented in this structured way to facilitate their use in real business situations.

The tools and techniques of Level 1 provide a sound foundation for businesses in general. They must be understood and widely used in a business before moving on to Level 2. Similarly, any business trying to adopt, adapt and follow techniques in Level 3 would be well advised to be fully conversant with the tools and techniques of Levels 1 and 2. Practical experience has shown that, if a business wants to perform at a high level, then the basics of good operational performance need to be secure, throughout all areas of the business, from first customer contact, through design, manufacturing, administration and finance to final servicing of the product.

The tools and techniques presented in this book have been tried, tested and proven over the past five years with a number of Irish-owned and Irish-managed businesses, from many different sectors. This work formed the basis for a thesis, which led to the award of a doctoral degree to Richard Keegan. The final section of this book provides some insight into the relevance of the research in the context of Ireland today and the challenges it faces in terms of building long-term sustainability and competitiveness.

LEVEL 1

LEVEL 3

Process Benchmarking: Chapter 21	The Five Ss: Chapter 22	Total Productive Maintenance: Chapter 23	Overall Equipment Efficiency: Chapter 24
Six Sigma: Chapter 25	Business Excellence: Chapter 26	Value Management, Analysis & Engineering: Chapter 27	Lean Production: Chapter 28
Target Cost Management: Chapter 29			

LEVEL 2

Facilitated Assessment benchmarking: Chapter 7	Physical & Process Flow in the Office: Chapter 8	Physical & Process Development: Chapter 8	Production Control Systems: Chapter 9
Saving Time: Chapter 10	Maintenance: Chapter 11	Practical Quality: Chapter 12	Teams & Team-Building: Chapter 13
World Class Sales: Chapter 14	Financial Management: Chapter 15	Supply Chain & Logistics: Chapter 16	Innovation & Design: Chapter 13
ABC & Strategy: Chapter 18	Implementation: Chapter 19		

LEVEL 1

Self Assessment benchmarking: Chapter 5	**Physical Flow: Chapter 5**	**Process Flow: Chapter 5**	**Set-Up Time Reduction: Chapter 5**
Basic Maintenance: Chapter 5	**Check Sheets: Chapter 5**	**Run Charts: Chapter 5**	**People & Teams: Chapter 6**

4: First Steps

Where to start? The tools and techniques presented in Level 1 act as a foundation, a base from which to build. The tools are organised to provide a practical, supportive approach to operational improvement. A business aiming to improve its performance, effectiveness and efficiency should want to progress on to Levels 2 and 3, but it must master the tools and techniques at Level 1 first. Managers and workers will be more able to easily absorb and use Level 2 and 3 tools, if they have mastered the tools and techniques of Level 1.

The tools are presented in an ordered way to help you use them quickly and effectively. By starting with the Physical Flow and Process Flow tools, you are focused naturally onto the operations that you know, and are helped to see them in a new light. This new approach to the commonplace usually leads to people achieving early gains and positive results as they improve their own processes. This leads to positive reinforcement and a desire to tackle the next challenge.

Simple but essential concepts of set-up-time reduction and basic maintenance are followed by some highly useful quality tools known as check sheets and run charts.

Level 1 concludes with an insight into one of the key areas of truly world class operators – people and teams.

5: WAR ON WASTE –
THE FIRST SKIRMISH

Waste is all around us in business. Not just the normal forms of waste that we are familiar with such as drafts of documents, incorrectly filled forms, damaged goods or incorrectly produced parts but waste as identified by Toyota Corporation.

When Toyota was faced with the need to improve their operations, it looked at what it was doing and identified seven basic wastes:

- Waste of motion within a workplace
- Transportation waste – moving from place to place
- Processing waste – using an under-developed processing system
- Waste from defects
- Waste from waiting time
- Waste from over-production – making more parts than necessary
- Inventory waste – having too many parts that can deteriorate or become obsolete.

Many of these wastes can be found in general business just as much as they can be found in manufacturing industry. For example, if one analyses the time it takes from the moment when a salesman takes an order to the time the order is delivered to the customer, it may be that the delays in order-processing or in generating shipping documents can equal, if not exceed, the manufacturing or processing time.

The key responses developed to meet these issues were outlined in the core WCB toolkit. Using these tools, one can find ways to improve performance by using:

- Teams to look actively at the processes being used
- Physical flow and process flow analysis
- Check sheets and run charts.

But what's next? How else can operations and processes be improved in a practical way?

Self Assessment

Self Assessment is the easiest and simplest form of benchmarking. It should be seen as a first step in objective diagnosis of the performance level of a business in an effort to prioritise improvement activities.

This type of benchmarking is easy to do. All that's needed your own performance figures and those of your competitors or sectoral averages/norms. For non-quantitative areas, one can answer a set of questions on the practices employed in the business.

The difficulty with Self Assessment is the "self" part. How many people can recognise their own failings? International experience shows that, where companies use Self Assessment, they tend to be overly positive in how they see their own performance.

However, given a positive attitude and a will to find ways to improve a business, Self Assessment can be a useful first step on the road to improved performance.

PHYSICAL FLOW

How do materials move through the production department? How many people work on each piece or job? How many different work areas does each job pass through? Why? These fundamental questions can be applied as easily to the office area – the only real difference is usually found in the distances travelled.

These questions underpin the need for physical flow analysis. In simple terms, physical flow analysis means looking at the physical movement of things within an operation. Sketching out the movements can often lead to questioning why things are done a particular way.

The first step in using the tool requires a sketch be made of the general layout of the area under investigation.

The second step requires the sketching of the physical movements of materials through the process. The resulting sketches became known as "spaghetti diagrams", for obvious reasons. Most operations are laid out in an efficient way when they are first installed. However, over time, and with changes of equipment or new people arriving, the physical layout of manufacturing and office areas can move away from the optimum.

A particular feature of the spaghetti diagram is that, at the end of each movement line, there is a build up of work-in-progress (WIP) – a bundle of invoices to be processed, a batch of orders to be entered or a box of parts to be machined. In any case, there is a build up, which provides the people working there with a degree of comfort that they have work to do. Managers like to see these piles of WIP, because they then know that their people have work to do. However, these piles of WIP are costly, in terms of time to process jobs as well as in terms of cash – to prove this, at each location on the sketch, simply note the value, in Euro, of the paperwork (invoices, orders, bills) or materials in the manufacturing area.

The key objective of the physical process flow exercise is to find ways to remove, or at least reduce, movements from the operation. A useful measure in an industrial environment can be how many tonne-kilometres of material are moved around the factory each year? In the office environment, how many kilometres is paper moved each year? Obviously, no customer willingly pays for these movements, so who is paying for them? The business is, because it is paying for these wastes of movement through a reduced margin. Lost profit pays for these wasteful kilometres and tonne kilometres.

As an example, let's look at a manufacturing process – door manufacture. A simplified sketch of the joinery, and the physical movement of parts and components through it, is shown in **Figure 6**. The layout has been simplified by reducing the number of individual machines in the area, by not showing WIP stocks or materials stored on the production floor, and by omitting the movement of operators.

A quick way of achieving a similar insight – before going to the trouble of committing it all to paper – is to stand on a balcony, up a stairs, or in some other place where an overview of the place can be seen. People are often surprised at the impact made by looking at their operation from this unusual perspective.

FIGURE 6: PHYSICAL FLOW DIAGRAM - JOINERY

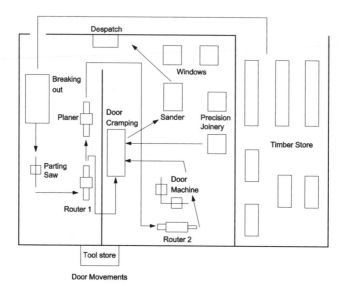

The next tool in the core toolkit is linked closely to the physical flow analysis tool – it is process flow analysis.

PROCESS FLOW

This tool is designed to help people see and understand what is happening in their operation and also to help determine the theoretical optimum that could be achieved (see **Figure 7**).

Back in the 1950s and 1960s, most managers came from the shop floor, from having "done the job". They understood the details of the work their staff were doing because they had done it themselves. Nowadays, however, managers frequently do not have the practical experience held by their staff – we have come to rely more on education rather than experience. In many ways, this has been a positive development, allowing companies to move up the value chain but, in some cases, managers have lost contact with the realities in the operations area. You may think that you know what happens in the office or on the shop floor but, frequently, this knowledge is at best cursory and often wide of the mark.

This knowledge gap is important, if you are trying to improve a process. Before you can identify areas for improvement, you need to know exactly what is happening. This is an ideal task for a newly-created team, which can map the process in their own areas and, together, build a complete map of the process. At this stage, this exercise should be carried out without judgement as to whether a particular step is adding value or not. The primary aim is to capture the true facts of what is happening in the operation.

FIGURE 7: PROCESS FLOW – JOINERY

Steps in process:
    Move from Timber Store to Breaking Out
    Break out
    Move to Pointing Saw
    Move to Router 1
    Large parts to Planer
    Small parts lifted and carried by operator to Door Cramping
    Large parts to Router 2
    Parts to Door Machine
    To Door Cramping
    Door assembly
    Doors moved to Sander
    Finished doors moved to Despatch

Note 1:
After each move, the parts waited to be worked on. Large levels of WIP were evident, as well as significant numbers of staff walking to get parts, materials and tools.
Note 2:
This process refers to door manufacture. The operation also produced windows and "precision joinery" (bespoke one-off specials).
Note 3:
The layout has been simplified, as has the process, to try to aid understanding.

The second part of the exercise is to determine the theoretical optimum process – what *should* be happening. The team can brainstorm this part of the exercise.

The real challenge is to make the actual process used as close as possible to the theoretical optimum. Once the actual steps of the process have been captured and the theoretical optimum has been determined, the team can move towards reducing the wasteful, non-value-added steps. They should focus on identifying the value-adding steps – a suggestion is to use a green highlighter to identify value-adding steps and red one to highlight non-value-added ones.

The close links between the physical and process flow tools should be clear now. The physical analysis can help highlight improvement opportunities.

In this particular business, the joinery operation had grown over the years, new machines and new processes had been added, often wherever a small bit of space could be found. The business was under extreme pressure to produce more product, as its customers were very happy with the high quality. However, the layout had come to impose severe restrictions on the business' ability to produce. The physical and process flow diagrams immediately made clear wastes that could, and needed to, be tackled and removed. Working as a team of owner-manager, production manager, lead hand and machine operators, the joinery devised a revised layout, shown in **Figure 8**.

FIGURE 8: DEVELOPED PROCESS FLOW - JOINERY

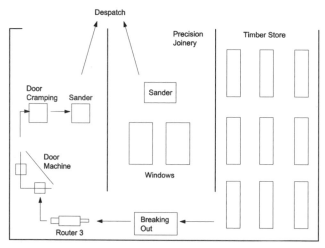

The new layout allowed the joinery to use the feed-out of one machine as the feed-in to the next. Movements of men and materials was significantly reduced. Tools required for use in a specific area, or on a particular machine, were stored close by using a "shadow board". The key point of the new layout is that output increased.

This arrangement, where activity for a given product or component is centred in a single area, is known as Cellular Manufacturing, since machines are organised in cells and work pieces flow naturally from one machine to the next, with the objective of completing a finished part or product within each cell.

Case Study:
Burnside Autocyl Ltd

Burnside is a 25-year-old engineering company involved in the production of hydraulic cylinders, primarily for the automotive sector, with its main customer base in Germany.

Two years ago, prior to the implementation of WCB, the company suffered from high raw material stock levels, a traditional clock-in time-recording system, WIP stocks booked through only one location, and all staff were hired by the managing director.

The management structure is now flat, with team leaders reporting directly to the managing director and being responsible for their own customer base. Team leaders take orders directly from customers and deal with issues and problems as they arise. There is no production manager in the business! Cell leaders (all former operators) have developed to the point where they are all equivalent to production managers in their own areas, with the power to hire staff as needed. The managing director has worked hard to develop the abilities he saw in his staff and has created a young vibrant management team.

At the start of its World Class process, Burnside had very little benchmarking in place at cell level. Now, staff use charts and check sheets in the cells to monitor progress and to identify key areas requiring improvement. Burnside has also widened its search for best practice using benchmarking:

- All staff on the production floor have participated in visits to Irish factories, some customers, suppliers and outside industry.

- Burnside now benchmarks with a large US company, in Texas. Visits to and from the US have led to a strategic alliance with them, with both sides learning from each other. Future plans include swapping people to build capabilities in both businesses.

The Improvement Process

Three working groups were formed initially. Individually, each group made some progress but largely operated as satellites, not really getting involvement of all the team leaders. They decided to re-focus, and reduced teams to only two people in each cell, with a "floating" member.

Results

The benefits of the process to the company were:
- Raw materials reduced by 50%.
- WIP down by 25%.
- WIP accuracy in cells up by 50%.
- Stock turnover up from 3 times a year to 5. Stock now booked to cells.
- Have 5 cell leaders, who run cells as separate businesses.
- Staff hired, trained and fired by cell leaders.
- People check in, not using time clocks, with the cell leader recording times and costs.

SET-UP TIME REDUCTION

In order to process single unit orders, change-over from one job to another must be accomplished with a minimum of fuss, just as one switches from a wordprocessor to a spreadsheet on a PC. However, in a manufacturing environment, change-over is often time-consuming and always loses production. Thus, it is often easier for production staff to produce long runs of the same, input them into storage and draw from the stores as needed. Although convenient for production staff, the downside to this approach is that it is very demanding of production time and invariably leads to long lead times, high levels of stock and, often, to obsolescence of that stock due to market changes or waste due to deterioration of products while in storage. In addition, the marketplace increasingly demands greater variety, which increases the need to be able to produce small quantities – even individual products. To meet these demands, set-up-times must be reduced to the level where time lost on change-over is negligible.

The task of reducing set up time can be tackled like other WCB tasks. First, it is essential to know what is actually involved in the change-over before beginning to find ways of improving it. Recording on video what happens during a change-over provides a permanent record, ensuring that all steps in the process are captured.

The fundamentals of reducing set-up-time are based on the identification of *internal* and *external* tasks (see **Figure 9**).

- **Internal tasks:** Those that can only be performed when the machine or process is stopped – replacement of tooling, moulds, etc.

- **External tasks:** Those that can be performed while the machine is still running – getting parts and tools ready, locating materials, initial settings, general preparations, etc.

FIGURE 9: CHANGE-OVER TIME

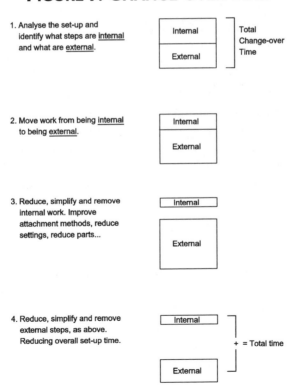

Once what happens during the change-over has been recorded, the set-up improvement team can identify wastes and areas for improvement. The use of standardised tooling, quick release mechanical and electrical connectors, standardised datum points and many other points of detailing can have a significant impact in reducing overall set-up-time. Industry journals and sales brochures for the latest machinery can often be used to help the team see new ways of achieving their objective.

When a better, shorter and simpler way of performing the set-up has been arrived at, record it. Train all relevant staff on the new way of working and ensure that this approach is followed.

But remember, the quickest and best change-over and the easiest one to perform is the set-up that is not done. If product design can remove the need for a component, then it is not necessary to make it or change-over from making another part to make it. If planning can plan efficiently, and sales can sell a relatively standardised product range, then the need for change-overs is minimised.

BASIC MAINTENANCE

How can we expect machines or processes to produce high quality goods as required, if the machinery is not maintained properly?

The Total Productive Maintenance (TPM) concept takes the pragmatic approach that, to make good products, one needs to be able to rely on one's machines. When you start a job, you want to be able to finish it, without having to fix a machine during the job. TPM uses check sheets and run charts to help identify where, and why, machines break down. The next step is to use teams to develop the machines to the point where they no longer break down.

Much of this approach is basic engineering practice, but applied to a very high degree of intensity. Operators are trained in machine maintenance, they clean and lubricate their own machines, they know the standard operating conditions of the machine and they also are trained to recognise when something is going wrong. Remember when you rode a bicycle? It was usually easier to tighten the chain before it fell off and jammed the sprocket than to ignore it, release and fix it and then tighten it *after* it jammed. The same rule applies in industry: if a problem is caught before it jams a machine, it is generally easier to address.

By using the TPM approach, leading companies are not only "addressing before jams" but are also developing machines to the point where they will not jam. This effort has resulted in major benefits. Machines are capable of running, unattended, in unlit factories, where materials are fed in at one end and products arrive out the other. The cost/benefit of being able to run a shift unattended is high. Much of the effort required to achieve this is basic, using well-proven ideas and concepts.

Although it was developed in Japan, TPM is not only a Japanese phenomenon or even a modern one. In the Husquvarna Museum in Jonkoping, Sweden, is an example of a machine built in the early 1900s which consists of eight machining stages, each fed automatically from the previous one, designed to turn tubes of steel into finished rifle barrels, using water-wheel-driven leather belts as a drive system

A striking feature of walking through Japanese factories is that much of their equipment is 10 to 20 years old, but very well maintained and sporting much of the latest measuring equipment, digital controls and early warning systems, all retrofitted. The effort and the cash have gone into developing capability rather than buying shiny new machines.

After operators have been trained in the basics of maintenance, it is often useful to train maintenance staff in the operation of machines. Through this exercise, both teams can understand the challenges facing the other and can begin to develop innovative solutions to problems.

There are a number of types of maintenance:

1. Fixed time maintenance
2. Condition-based maintenance
3. Opportunity maintenance
4. Operate to failure
5. Design out maintenance.

Which type of maintenance approach a business chooses to follow will depend on its particular circumstances, what type of equipment it has and what resources it can allocate to the maintenance area. At Level 1 of ABC, we look at fixed time maintenance I this chapter and the other forms of maintenance in **Chapter 11** under Level 2.

Fixed Time Maintenance

As the name implies, this maintenance takes place based on time. Daily, weekly, monthly or yearly checks, adjustments and replacements are made, to ensure that the machine performs at its optimum. Parts are changed before they reach the end of their service life. By doing this, there is a high probability that the machine will operate faultlessly between services. The time between changing components and parts is based on design information and experience. The system is best known in the automotive world where oil, filters and plugs are changed according to time or mileage criteria.

In industry, it is often difficult to assemble sufficient data to know when parts are approaching the end of their service lives – this can mean that some parts are replaced unnecessarily. The more complex the machine, the harder it is to be accurate in replacement schedules.

Now that we have looked at the basic tools of operational improvement, we will now move on to look at the basic quality tools of Level 1 Applied Benchmarking for Competitiveness.

CHECK SHEETS

We need to improve. We want to improve. What is holding us back?

If one asks staff for the cause of lost production, or delays in providing service to customers, or the reasons for defects, quite often the reason given is not, in fact, the real reason for poor performance. It is an "opinion", not a "fact".

The check sheet is one of the simplest quality tools and one of the most powerful. When faced with the task of improving a process, the challenge is often in knowing what is actually happening as the process runs – what are the facts of the situation rather than people's opinions, since opinions and instinct can be wrong. The check sheet provides a simple way to record the facts of the situation.

Case Study:
Killala Precision Components Ltd

Killala Precision Components Limited is an industrial sub-contract machining company. Formed in 1981, it now occupies a 20,000 sq. ft. plant and employs 60 staff. It produces high quality precision-turned components in many different materials and has shown a continuous record of growth and achievement.

It operates up to 40 machines, with management reports providing high levels of information on individual machine efficiencies. Management identified the need to increase productivity in the face of increasing competition.

Check Sheets

The company introduced check sheets to capture information that could be used to reduce losses and improve efficiency. The check sheets allowed operators and management to identify the root causes of losses. Management, machine operators, maintenance and engineering design staff then moved to address the issues identified. Productivity increased significantly as a result.

If faced with improving a sales operation, some basic facts are needed:

- Who is buying what?
- When?
- In what quantities?
- From which sales people?

If one's focus is on improving an administration group's effectiveness and efficiency, it is probably important to know:

- Who is accurate in their work and who is not?
- What types of interruptions occur?
- At what frequency?

If one's focus is on the performance of a manufacturing area, it may be necessary to know:

- Why machines stop?
- How often does this happen?
- How long do the interruptions to production last?

These and many other questions are easily captured using check sheets. A check sheet captures facts without imposing a significant workload, by recording, using a simple mark on the sheet, of the number and types of errors in a process or in a product.

When developing a check sheet, consider:

- What is to be recorded?

- Over what time period?
- Who will record the data?
- Who will act on the data to improve the process?

The fourth step is probably the most important. If time and energy are spent in capturing and recording data, then action to improve the process afterwards is necessary. Otherwise, the exercise is simply an additional waste.

As an example, let's look at an administration case in **Figure 10**, where a check sheet captures data on the process.

FIGURE 10: ADMINISTRATION CHECK SHEET

Source of Work	
Telephone	| | | |
Visitor	| | |
E-mail	| | | | | |
New Query	|
Rework	| |
Other	|
Person	
Date	

By looking at the check sheets for all staff in the group, one can determine whether there are problems with telephone-answering or the handling of visitors. Any improvements would then be based on facts.

There are some basic mistakes that people can make when they try to capture data from their operations. One key mistake is expecting workers to write down the reasons and causes for losses, of time or product. Few workers like to spend time writing, so little data is captured. Few managers, in turn, like to sift through mounds of paper to find out what happened. A check sheet both removes the need to write down causes of stoppages or interruptions and makes it easier to analyse the data captured.

A difficulty encountered by companies starting to use check sheets is that they tend to over-complicate, by adding too many items to the list. Experience has shown that six to seven items – one of which should be

"Other" – is an optimum. Obviously, if "Other" has many marks recorded against it, the list needs to be developed further to capture more useful information.

In analysing the data from a check sheet, do not assume that, because something happens most frequently, it is the most important problem – it is merely the most frequent and, because of that, deserving of attention. But one must gauge the impact of each fault to determine what, in fact, are the key issues identified by the check sheet.

Case Study:
C & C Springs

The company, based in Walkinstown, Dublin, had entered the computer business, using its expertise in spring materials and tooling design to make the spring steel shutters of 3.5" floppy disks. The process was being run over two shifts and operators were using a diary as a logbook to capture information on problems encountered. The supervisor checked the diary each morning but tended to make little use of the data recorded. The operators and toolmakers, skilled people, tended to focus on fire-fighting and responding to problems as they arose.

As part of the company's WCB process, a simple check sheet was developed, to capture data from the process without asking the operators to spend time writing (see **Figure 11**).

FIGURE 11: SAMPLE CHECK SHEET

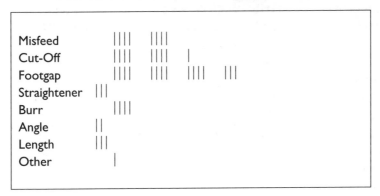

The tick marks represent each time the problem occurred. After a week's use, the data recorded was examined by the team, to see whether it was a true picture of the types of problems they had been encountering.

Remembering the point made earlier about check sheet analysis, the team checked the level of impact of each occurrence by looking at the time lost for each problem, and entered this information into its analysis of the check sheet, as shown in **Figure 12**.

FIGURE 12: ANALYSIS OF CHECK SHEET DATA 1

FAULT	NO. OF OCCURRENCES	TIME LOST
Misfeed	10	50
Cut-Off	11	20
Footgap	18	52
Straightener	03	90
Burr	04	130
Angle	02	42
Length	03	17
Other	01	05

When analysing check sheets, one tends to rank the data in terms of number of occurrences. One should also look at the impact of individual occurrences, as in **Figure 13**.

FIGURE 13: ANALYSIS OF CHECK SHEET DATA 2

Ordered by Time Lost:	TIME LOST	Ordered by Number of Occurrences:	NO. OF OCCURRENCES
Burr	130	Footgap	18
Straightener	90	Cut-Off	11
Footgap	52	Misfeed	10
Misfeed	50	Burr	4
Angle	42	Straightener	3
Cut-Off	20	Length	3
Length	17	Angle	2
Other	5	Other	1

If the company had simply ordered the data by occurrence, it would have failed to prioritise the "Burr" issue for attention. Care needs to be exercised when using these tools to ensure that people "see" what they are "looking" at when trying to "understand" the data, and what the data is saying about the process.

RUN CHART

The run chart presents trends over time. If an improvement process is underway, one hopes to see improvement over time, either in increased productivity or sales or in reduced defects and complaints.

Many companies do not record their performance over time – in effect, every day is another day in the mines for their staff. There is no means of knowing whether their performance is getting better, staying the same, or even deteriorating.

Run charts can be used to monitor performance on areas that are important to the business. If customers value on-time deliveries, then use a run chart to measure performance in this key area. If customers value response time, or accuracy in paperwork, performance in these areas should be measured over time. These measures should then be made available to the people who can affect change.

> There is no harm in letting people see what they have done
> – and what they have to do.
> **Denis Keegan**

With the simple inclusion of a target line, the run chart is not only a record of what performance has been achieved but also a challenge to all to reach the target. It is now a simple, but effective, motivator.

A run chart displays trends over time. It can be difficult to remember last week's performance, never mind performance two months ago. The run chart is most often used to record sales levels, production outputs or complaints received but can be used for any measure that can change over time. As an exercise, see whether you can visualise what the numbers in **Figure 14** show.

Then, look at the same data presented in a run chart, in **Figure 15**. Now, changes in performance can be seen clearly. If performance deteriorates, then questions can be asked to find out why. On a more positive note, if people have been working to improve a process, they will be able to see an improvement in performance on the run chart. This can act as a very positive reinforcement for the team.

FIGURE 14: MILES PER GALLON - TABLE

Fill No	Date	Km	Sum Km	Litres	Station	€	MPG
1	30-Oct			21.7	ST	11.98	
2	02-Nov	277		20.8	E	11.42	37.8
3	05-Nov	285	562	21.0	T	12.53	38.5
4	09-Nov	250	813	20.2	ST	11.17	35.2
5	11-Nov	267	1,081	19.2	E	11.36	39.5
6	14-Nov	312	1,394	20.8	ST	12.67	42.7
7	24-Nov	218	1,612	21	E	11.57	29.5
8	25-Nov	304	1,916	20.	T	11.99	41.8
9	03-Dec	244	2,161	19.5	SH	11.51	35.6
10	04-Dec	253	2,415	16.4	E	10.14	43.7
11	04-Dec	340	2,756	21.8	E	12.08	44.3
12	09-Dec	272	3,028	20.7	ST	12.05	37.3
13	17-Dec	268	3,297	21.6	E	11.72	35.2
14	22-Dec	198	3,495	19.4	ST	10.46	29.0
15	02-Feb	221	3,717	20.9	E	11.26	30.1
16	03-Feb	291	4,009	20.3	E	10.77	40.7
17	03-Mar	208	4,217	20.0	ST	10.55	29.6
18	16-Mar	217	4,435	19.3	E	10.38	32.0
19	23-Mar	255	4,691	20.2	E	10.98	35.9
20	25-Mar	269	4,961	19.7	SH	10.78	38.7
21	13-Apr	242	5,203	21.0	E	12.40	32.8
22	15-Apr	259	5,463	20.0	T	12.07	36.7
23	15-Apr	270	5,734	19.4	T	11.07	39.6
24	16-Apr	251	5,986	19.8	M	10.90	36.0

FIGURE 15: MILES PER GALLON - RUN CHART 1

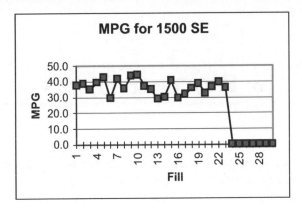

The run chart can be further developed as a challenge to the team. The addition of a target line will give the team an objective, and also the means to measure progress towards this objective, as in **Figure 16**.

FIGURE 16: MILES PER GALLON - RUN CHART 2

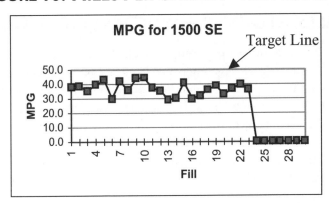

Using run charts with target lines, and highlighting key actions taken to secure improvement, may also help to develop an innovation culture in the business. The ever-present challenge is to ask what can be done next to bridge the gap between present and potential performance.

6: PEOPLE & TEAMS

Tools and techniques are important but, if they are to benefit an operation, they need to be used and implemented by people. People need to be managed and to be involved in the improvement process, in order to maximise their contribution to the business. People need to be respected and appreciated by their businesses and their management. People need to be led and to participate in a process.

This chapter looks at some basic techniques to start this process of building people power and capability, based always on mutual respect, trust and effort.

SKILLS REGISTER – WHO HAVE YOU GOT?

Business depends on people. People work the systems, processes and machines that deliver customer needs. The skills, experiences and expertise of the people in a business will define the quality of product offering. But how can a business develop its people to allow it to operate at the highest levels of performance? The World Class approach places an emphasis on teams and team-working.

All teams are made up of individuals, with different abilities, personalities and experience levels. To develop a fully-capable team means identifying:

- What skills and experience are required by the business
- Who it has available
- What is their level of capability in relation to the required skills set.

It can be very difficult to identify individuals' abilities objectively. The World Class approach provides a tool known as the "skills register" to help with this process. An example of a skills register for administration and customer support is presented in **Figure 17**.

FIGURE 17: SKILLS REGISTER

Job Area: Administration and Customer Support

Job Details	Telephone		Computer Skills			Administration	
	Answer	Transfer	Word	Excel	Prop. System	Order Entry	Customer Complaints
Richard							
Paddy							
Mary							
Joan							

Each staff member has a four-box square under each of the key job skill areas. The skill level of each staff member is represented by the number of filled boxes. The standard interpretation of the skills register is shown in **Figure 18**.

FIGURE 18: INTERPRETATION OF SKILLS REGISTER

No Boxes: Staff-member is untrained or unskilled.

One Box: A basic introduction to the topic has been given.

Two Boxes: Staff-member is able to perform the task, under supervision and with support.

Three Boxes: Staff-member is largely capable of performing the task, although they may require some support and light supervision.

Four Boxes: Staff-member is fully capable.

The system is very simple: gaps in skills are easily seen and recognised and can be addressed.

The skills register is often used on an individual basis as part of personal development plans and can also be used in a more general way where the register is displayed in team meeting areas. This approach can be helpful where team members realise they have gaps in their skills that they can take training for.

TEAMS

Effective team-building is essential in today's highly competitive working environment. The power of a well-functioning team can be the difference between success and failure. Most companies can afford to buy or lease good equipment and machines. The difference between successful and unsuccessful companies often lies in how well they use these assets. The people working in a business or organisation add the value to its products or services. If people in a business do not work together, then the business will be open to attack from its competitors. In the developing knowledge-based economic environment, those businesses that harness the potential of their people will thrive, those that do not will find it difficult to survive.

We know this harnessing of individuals as building teams. There are clear and effective ways of bringing people together, to work together, for a common objective. This is the central point in relation to team building – people need to have a common objective, a reason to work as a team, a goal. One can often see volunteers doing work, for free, that they would never do if they were being paid, because they are working to achieve an objective, a shared goal.

Case Study:
Dingle Lamps

Louis Mulcahy, initially operating from premises in Dublin, founded the company in 1974. He subsequently moved to Ballyferriter, Co Kerry, from where he continued to grow the business. The business has managed to retain its craft ethos, despite its growth. Its products are hand-thrown with a particular emphasis on large pieces. These are particularly difficult to master and the operation has earned a good reputation for its expertise in this area. The company employed 35 staff at the start of its World Class initiative, and now employs over 60, with both throwing and sales operations on the one site.

Key Issues
The level of formal supervisory skill and training within the business was low, and certainly not at a self-sustaining level. The level of systems in both administration and manufacturing areas was not sufficient to manage the business without the advantage of years of experience. And

finally, the need existed to augment the management team with complementary skills to the owner/manager.

The starting point for this stage of the company's development efforts was to look at current and future management structures, with a view to identifying key staff for key positions. It became clear that:

- There were clear gaps in the structure, in particular at the administration and production management levels
- The supervisory level was untrained and had not had the opportunity to develop capability in this area.

In addition to these structural difficulties, the management clearly identified the need to continue to develop the business' manufacturing capability as well as its sales efforts.

Structural Development

Louis Mulcahy developed a list of priorities or action points to form the basis for his action plan. An off-site two-day session was arranged for the supervisory and senior level of management. At this session, the strategic plan developed by the MD was presented for discussion.

Three clear discussion themes were presented to the supervisors under the headings of quality, productivity and reject levels. The supervisors broke into discussion groups and identified specific actions they needed to adopt in their own specific areas to meet the demands of the overall strategic plan. Within months, as a team, the supervisors developed an agreed company plan, broken down by production areas, setting targets and rates of production for their respective areas. They had analysed the sales by volume and value and were moving to address issues and problems identified. They had also classified the product range according to difficulty to make and had examined the relative skills of the throwers against the product range classification system. This ensured that unskilled staff were not allocated to work they were unsuited to do, while also giving the throwers a progression ladder for advancement. Effectively, the supervisors developed operational plans to meet the objectives of the overall business plan, and they now had a common goal and an objective to achieve.

Results Achieved

The company achieved its objectives of securing and developing a core of capable supervisors, managing professionally, improving profitability and growing sales and jobs.

Sales were increased by circa 7%, with a heightened focus on profitable lines and customers. And finally, staff numbers increased.

The same point applies in business. For people to work together as a team, there needs to be a reason to do so. Just bringing people together and calling them a team will not deliver teamwork. It is essential that a real reason exists, or is created, for them to work together. Without this reason, they will continue to work as they had before – as individuals. The introduction of a shared objective, one that cannot be achieved by individual action, is useful to get the attention of all concerned.

A key factor for success, when trying to form a team in a business environment, is that management show an ongoing interest in the activities of the team, as well as in the progress and results of the team. Unless people see that their efforts are both significant and important, they are unlikely to put much effort into developing this alien form of working. On the other hand, if management show an interest in the effort, if they monitor progress and introduce measures to ensure team working is happening, people will respond and deliver on the benefits of team-working.

There is a lot known about the detail of team-building. Many larger organisations and businesses employ such techniques as psychometric profiling, personality profiling and other psychological tools and techniques to ensure they have a good mix of characteristics in a team. Most small and medium-sized companies do not have this luxury, and have a restricted pool of people to choose from.

So, is it possible to form effective teams without using the specialist tools and techniques? The answer is Yes! Once the reason for the team to exist has been identified, and the objective that needs to be reached has been set, the process of team building can begin. However, on a practical note, it is important to recognise that not everybody is able or suited to working in a team environment. Some people find it very difficult to interact with others. The decision must be made as to whether such individuals have a positive role to play within the organisation, working on their individual tasks or whether their best opportunities lie outside the organisation. These can be difficult decisions for all concerned. People in general fall into a number of categories:

- **Type A:** Those who are inherently positive, who will try to deliver, who will take on new challenges and new ideas. These account for about 10% of a workforce.

- **Type B:** The main body of people in a workforce, at both management and operational levels, accounting for about 85% of the workforce. These people want to see how things will work out before they commit to a new way of working. When, and if, they see the new way working, they are usually happy to join in.

- **Type C:** The negative group, those who always seem to say "That won't work!" Quite often these are experienced people, with lots of skill and ability. Maybe they are right, maybe the new way won't work, because they have seen a serious flaw. Maybe they also see a solution to the flaw! This can be a hard group to win over but also a very rewarding one. Unfortunately, experience has shown that while many within this group can and do change to be positive contributors, some of these people find it impossible to embrace change and generally tend to pursue alternative careers.

So, Where to Start?

It is important to identify a problem or issue for the team that will be both challenging and achievable. It needs to be challenging enough to allow people to feel that they have contributed to its solution and also needs to be achievable within a reasonable timescale. If the problem or issue is too big or too difficult, then the team may fail, with ongoing negative repercussions on future improvement activities.

Once the issue or problem has been identified, it is time to identify who should be on the team. We will deal later with the selection of team members, at this point we are dealing only with the types of people to be on the team: A, B or C.

Practical experience has shown that the first efforts at team-building are the most important. If introducing team-working to help an improvement initiative, it is probably best to pick positive, Type A people, with some Type B "wait and see" people in the early teams.

Some experts suggest including Type C people, the "nay sayers", in early teams. We believe that this is not the most effective approach. It is usually better to achieve success with a positive or neutral group of people rather than trying to convince the "nay sayers" to change their attitude.

Case Study:
ColourBooks Ltd

COLOURBOOKS LTD.

Colour Books started operations in 1990 because the
managing director and his chairman believed there was a
need to print books in Ireland. At the time, the commonly-
held belief was that it was impossible to print books
profitably in Ireland. The drive and vision of the
management team helped them to identify a way that they could
compete with book printers from overseas. Effectively, they re-designed
the process of printing books and designed their operations to meet the
full requirements of publishers in an effective and efficient way. Based on
this effort at Business Process Re-engineering, the company was a leader
from the beginning!

Over the following seven years, the competition in Ireland came to
realise that the book-printing business could be profitable and took
their own steps to move into the market. The management team
decided, therefore, that they needed to look at the basics of their
operation, if they were to secure the future of the business in the face
of this increasing competition.

One of the projects launched was in the Print Room area, focussing on
maintenance and effectiveness of machinery using teamwork.

Print Room
*   Put in place Kanban for inks.
*   Tool chests with marked shadow boards.
*   Painted floor.
*   Upgraded housekeeping.
*   Set up a team, focused on equipment and downtime.
*   A Continuous Improvement board was located behind each
    machine. Printers and assistants could put problems on the board as
    they occurred.
*   Bought a second set of rollers/machine, allowing machines to run
    while the first set was being cleaned.

It took some time for all printers to join the process. The company
started with two machines first; as the continuous improvement process
went on, other machine operators became disgruntled and wanted to
get involved. So, the rest of the printers were taken on board.

Results of WCB for the company

After the implementation of the WCB programme, the following changes were in place:

- Downtime reduced from 15 hours to 5 hours per week.
- Overall performance at 50% better than PIRA industry standard.
- £17,000 savings in pre-press costs.
- Regular team meeting held.
- Suggestions acted upon and monitored - Continuous Improvement board.
- Kanban system in place.
- Everything in its place and a place for everything - All tools have a home.
- Housekeeping to a very high standard.
- Problems quantified, analysed and addressed.
- Proper training plan put in place.
- Working with the customer to identify their needs.
- Greater control over work.

The Facilitator

Team-working can be a new way of working for many people. How do they do it? How is it different from what went before? These and many more questions can – and do – arise.

A facilitator can be very helpful when introducing team-working, providing answers to many questions and helping people to come to terms with the new approach. The facilitator can be a member of staff or an outsider. Either approach can be successful. Many companies and organisations choose to use an external facilitator in the early stages, taking the opportunity to learn from experienced people and also maybe to benefit from somebody outside the organisation "breaking the ice." The outsider can often raise issues and questions that would be difficult for someone within the operation. This can be particularly useful where deep-seated issues exist.

The role of the facilitator can be difficult and is frequently taxing, as they have to retain a degree of separation from the company and the issues, while concentrating very closely on them and the team process to help ensure a positive outcome. The facilitator has been likened to a catalyst in a chemical reaction, not strictly necessary for the reaction to take place but helpful in ensuring the result and speeding the process. The catalyst helps bring about change without being changed itself.

Once the general objective and goals of the team have been identified and the team members selected, typically the facilitator's role involves:

- Leading the first team meeting
- Helping the team select detailed projects to deliver on the objectives
- Starting the process of open discussion
- Ensuring that all team members get the opportunity to contribute
- Letting the team set its own priorities
- Moving away by devolving power and authority to the team
- Monitoring the progress of the team towards its objectives
- Praising and reinforcing achievements
- Identifying areas where additional effort are required
- Withdrawing, leaving a functioning team in place.

As people become confident in the team-working environment, the power of the team develops. People's confidence builds naturally as they begin to see the success of their efforts, as they see the results of their teamwork. People can often be surprised at their team's effectiveness, as they find solutions to issues and problems that have often been worked around or ignored for a long time.

It is clear that there are many different cultures in place in business, industry and the general public and private sectors. Not everyone works in an open environment where ideas and suggestions are welcomed, acknowledged or rewarded. In the more extreme cases, where an autocratic style of management exists, the facilitator must work to protect the newly developing team. They must try to find space for the team to start delivering on its potential by keeping the autocratic manager informed of its development and its efforts. The facilitator may also need to protect the team from over-expectation – where people assume the simple creation of a team will deliver immediate and dramatic results.

The role of the facilitator is a delicate and important one, demanding a high level of inter-personal skills and judgement. A key task for the facilitator is to withdraw from the team, leaving the team with the skill, understanding and ability to be self-sustaining.

Respect

The most important aspect of team-building is both the most obvious and often the most forgotten – respect. It is in how we respect others, their different skills, characteristics and abilities that we demonstrate true commitment to team-working. Without this fundamental of mutual respect, there is no real prospect of a successful, sustainable team being developed. One must recognise individual contributions as well as contributions to the overall goals and objectives of the business.

TEAM EVOLUTION

Psychologists have studied the dynamics of teams over many years and have identified four clear stages in team evolution:

- Forming
- Storming
- Norming
- Performing.

Forming

A group of people is not a team – however, a group of people brought together with a common objective or task can be brought quickly to form a team.

Once the group is brought together, team dynamics begin to take over. People look to see who else is there, why they have been asked to participate and why others are there or not there, as the case may be.

As the work progresses, in most organisations, a degree of normal business manners is evident. Most groups want to try to be good, to achieve the goals and objectives set for them and there is a generally high level of morale and good spirits. In the autocratic company, teams can be slower to form, with people more careful in how they contribute and what they say. People will often wait to see what and how the "boss" approaches the activity. If the boss is clearly supportive of the effort, and responds positively to the contributions of individuals, then this will lead to a self re-inforcing outcome. If the boss is seen to be negative, then the process is probably doomed to failure or at best a difficult life.

At the first team meeting, the tasks and objectives of the team are introduced and, while they may be agreed as achievable, there is often little sense of ownership of the issues. Depending on the make-up of the team, there may even be some difficulty in them understanding the extent of the problems or the depth of the issues. Usually though, the team members will feel that it is possible to find solutions.

The question of team leadership is often raised. Who should lead the team and how is this person chosen? In most situations in small and medium-sized companies, the leader is self-evident. Where a facilitator is used, then it is usual for the facilitator either to lead the first meeting or to help the manager or chosen team leader to do so. The leader will help the team focus on its objectives, allocate specific tasks, decide when and where team meetings will need to take place to ensure progress is made and generally lead the newly-formed team.

Storming

As the name suggests, storming can be a difficult period for the team. By this stage, a number of meetings have taken place and some frustrations may have arisen. Some of the team will be happy with progress to date; others may feel that not enough has been done and that some team members are not committed enough to the tasks. People have come to *care* about the issues and tasks of the team. They have internalised the tasks and taken ownership of them. The team's problems are now *their* problems and they have committed to finding solutions. Team meetings can become quite involved, with forthright discussion and opposing suggestions for solutions being made.

At the same time, team members can often start to compete for position within the team, to move towards leadership positions or to align themselves with others. Quite often, the younger members of the team will lead in terms of levels of energy and enthusiasm and will start to get clear results for their efforts. This, in turn, can often lead to the energising of the more experienced team members.

The leader needs to manage the process carefully now, ensuring that high energy interactions do not degenerate into negativity and that the contributions of all members are recognised. It is also important to encourage all members to contribute. Often the quieter members can be shaded by the more outspoken members, although they often have valuable contributions to make to final solutions. The leader should be able to generate a level of mutual appreciation within the team. It should be clear that individuals have their own skills and attributes and a level of mutual respect starts to develop.

On the practical side of the team's work, some of the tasks set will be yielding to solutions, some will not. It is important to monitor progress and clearly identify which tasks are still posing problems. Can the team learn from their successes to help solve the outstanding issues? By focusing attention more clearly on the difficult tasks, the team will move to further develop its problem-solving abilities, to develop its internal capability. An effort needs to be made to come up with potential new ideas for problems, to fully understand the issues and take steps to develop solutions.

Throughout this time, the team leader's role is centrally important. They need to be focused on the big picture. How is the team moving towards their overall goal and objectives? Are all team members contributing? Is the level of commitment and energy to the tasks being shared equally? The leader's role will probably be a mixture of pushing and pulling, cajoling and controlling, bringing on the quieter members of the team and managing the enthusiasm of the young Turks. In some instances, the leader may need to be a conciliator, if confrontation arises.

Norming

The team has become a team. They have developed a sense of respect for each other, recognising their individual contributions to the successes they have achieved. Individuals have come to understand their role within the team and are comfortable with it. The team will move to defend itself against others. Members have a level of interest in the team and its activities and they tend to manage themselves to get on with the tasks set for them and even identify further activities and tasks.

Positive results are being achieved, and the original tasks set for the team have moved well towards completion. Elements that may have caused problems earlier will have been re-examined and alternative solutions suggested until resolutions were identified. The team can discuss issues openly, with a high degree of introduction and positive outcomes.

The team's work, and its achievements, are fully team achievements rather than those of the leader. With this evolution, the role of the leader changes, to being responsible for the further development of capability within the team. They need to help the team understand learning points and opportunities for further growth, as well as recognising achievements and ensuring the team receives recognition for its efforts.

Performing

The team is at the height of its powers. They have developed the ability to solve problems, to address issues in an effective and efficient way. The original tasks have been completed and the team has either identified more demanding tasks for themselves or been allocated other issues by management. People have developed a level of pride in the team and others within the business are aware of it and may want to join.

Discussion within the team can often be robust, but without the negativity of earlier times. Members know that all opinions are expressed from a positive point of view rather than to score points off each other. The team is happy to take on extra work and to provide feedback on problems and progress. The team has developed its own shell, with members being protective of the team and its members. No body wants to leave.

Further information on the mechanics of team management will be presented in the Level 2 WCB Toolkit section.

Now that teams are in place and have identified and addressed a number of key issues or problems facing the business or organisation, possibly following a benchmarking exercise, what other tools are they to be armed with?

We now move to look at the other core tools, that help give structure to the teams and help them to tackle objectively the issues and problems identified. Remembering that a core element of the ABC approach is to "look, see and understand," the next set of core tools will help people "see the wood for the trees", to progress their capabilities as their skills and experience grow.

LEVEL 2

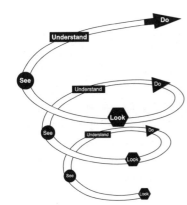

7: THE WORK CONTINUES

The fundamentals underpinning WCB are about providing a service or making a product: **Quicker, Better, Cheaper ...Together**. Often we see that where businesses work quicker, they are also better and consequently are cheaper. The key elements of WCB work together to deliver improved performance.

In Level 1, we looked at some basic, fundamentally important tools to help achieve effectiveness and efficiency. By now, people in the operation should be comfortable with working in a team, using quality tools such as check sheets and run charts to identify issues and monitor performance and they should have experience looking at the realities of processes.

At Level 2, we move to the next level of complexity. Many of the techniques presented here will be seen to be natural developments of the Level 1 tools. Others will be new and will demand effort to understand them and to make effective use of them. The challenge is the same for everyone in the business – "how to achieve sustainable businesses in the face of increasing competition".

The tools and techniques of Level 2 are presented in a series of small chapters. The order in which the tools are used is totally dependent on the business and the priorities identified at any given time. We will start with a development of the Physical and Process Flow tools, where the need to search continually for improvement is emphasised. We then look at different types of production control systems, discussing when each is appropriate. Next, we look at some simple time-saving approaches. Maintenance and the different approaches available are then addressed, before moving on to quality tools for the effective starting, running and improvement of processes.

The importance of supply chains and stock management, as well as the potential of clusters, is presented. Level 2 continues with a detailed and practical section on the mechanics of team-building and structural development. For businesses to be truly effective, they need to be able to sell their products or services. Level 2 contains a straightforward approach to developing sales, addressing forecasting and targeting and capturing new customers and sales. Understanding finance and some core measures and how they may help managers to understand and manage their operations is important. Equally, it is important to understand how bankers and potential investors view an operation, therefore the section provides some insights into financier's ratios.

Level 2 comes to an end with a section on building a strategy. Strategy is presented at the end of level 2, because most businesses are already in a chosen sector, with products, processes and customers. They can often improve the effectiveness and efficiency of the existing business more easily than they can move the business to a new area of operation. "Fix the existing operation first, then look to see where it might be taken" is good advice. Of course, in some circumstances, a business may find it appropriate to use the strategy chapter first.

Level 2 concludes with a suggested implementation approach.

Faciliatated Assessment

Note that, at Level 2, Faciliatated Assessment, rather than Self Assessment, is the appropriate benchmarking approach for companies at this stage of their development.

The introduction of a trained facilitator into the benchmarking process can greatly increase the level of objectivity. The facilitator will guide the company through the process, ensuring that all questions are fully explained and understood and that the company takes a realistic view of its capabilities and performance.

The facilitated approach can provide a good, simple, effective and secure introduction to international benchmarking. In Europe today, thousands of companies have undergone facilitated benchmarking exercises providing databases of information that is secure, comparable and truly international using the Microscope/Probe and Benchmark Index tools.

8: Lead-Time Reduction

One of the key measures used in a WCB implementation is that of Time.

Some European benchmarking colleagues who work for the UK's Inland Revenue discovered that, because the post was not opened until mid-day, staff were too late to make up a lodgement before the banks closed each day. This did not seem like a big matter until they realised that it was costing the Inland Revenue several million sterling each year. Needless to say, they now open the post first thing in the morning, with the appropriate staffing levels in place. Time is money!

Reducing Batch Sizes

Another key feature of WCB is the drive to reduce batch sizes. The optimum batch size is one unit, to ensure that no delays are encountered in a process or no WIP builds up.

Imagine a three-step process with five items to process, as shown in **Figure 19**. In the Batch Processing system, all items must be processed in area 1 before it can move to area 2, and all items must be processed in area 2 before moving to area 3. In the Single Item system, once a unit is produced in area A, it can be worked on in area B and, once completed there, it can be worked on in area C. If the processing time for each area for each unit is one minute, how long it will take to produce five items from each process?

Figure 19: Batch vs Single Item Production

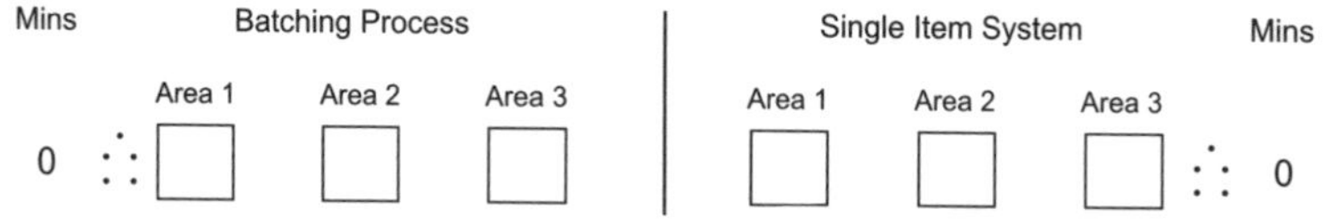

Take the time to work this. Then check your solution against **Figure 20**.

FIGURE 20: BATCH *VS* SINGLE ITEM PRODUCTION 2

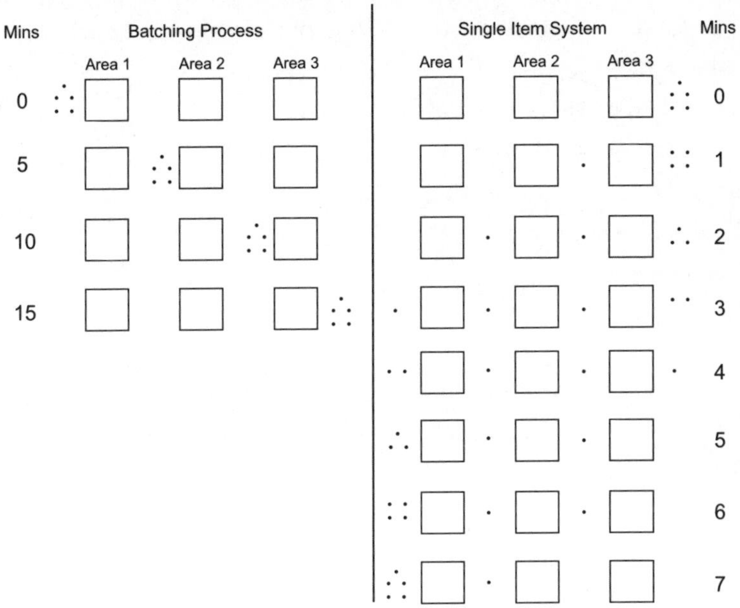

It is clear that the Single Item system needs very much less time to complete the work than the Batch Processing system. In addition, less WIP is created.

If the process is moved up to a continuous manufacturing system, major differences in WIP and incoming stock levels will also be seen.

Most importantly, the time to produce products or process paperwork is half that of the Batch Processing system. A single item system is the ideal – however, practical considerations may make this impossible to achieve today. But the same basic argument holds if batch size can be reduced from 100 units to 50, or 50 units to 20 or 20 to 10.

IN THE OFFICE

How can we use World Class Business tools in our offices, when we do not *make* anything in our offices? Although we are not cutting or welding metal, we are processing data, information and paperwork.

Let us look at how WCB works in an office environment using the tools we know.

The activity in offices can be best described and understood as processes, many of which are common to most businesses, such as:

- Order entry
- Accounts receivable
- Product or Service supply
- Personnel
- Financial accounting
- Accounts payable
- Purchasing.

There are other processes that only some companies have:

- R & D
- Marketing
- Sales
- Production
- Environmental monitoring.

Taking the order entry process as an example, let's start to map the process. Remember, we are looking for waste – waste is any action that adds cost but not value. Ask a simple question: Would you personally be prepared to pay your own money for all of the actions that are carried out in the process? Customers only want to pay for the added value, any added cost effectively reduces their profits.

In the office, forms of waste include:

- Counting
- Moving
- Looking for papers
- Reworking
- Filing
- Sorting
- Reconciling
- Checking
- Duplicating.

Let's see how we can use the Physical Flow and Process Flow analysis tools by working on an "Order Entry Process."

In an office environment, it's often easier to map the theoretical optimum process before recording the actual system in use. So let's start by mapping a theoretical system for entering an order into the system, as in **Figure 21**.

FIGURE 21: THEORETICAL ORDER ENTRY PROCESS

Receive order
Enter into sales order record
Check account status
Place order on production
Plan into production
Produce
Ship
Invoice

If the business is a distribution company, then rather than producing the product the process steps would refer to checking stock, and either delivering from stock or back ordering.

The process looks quite straightforward and logical. Now let us capture the actual process, by getting a team to map and record the steps involved in the process, as in **Figure 22**.

FIGURE 22: ACTUAL ORDER ENTRY PROCESS

Receive order – reception
To Sales office
Wait
Enter into sales record
To Finance
Wait
Clear account
To sales
Wait
To Production Planning
Wait
To Production
Produce
To Shipping
Documents to Administration
Check paperwork with Sales
Wait
Issue invoice

It is obvious that there are many more steps in the actual order entry process than in the theoretical optimum. It is also obvious that many of these additional steps are simply movements and waiting.

To help understand the implications of these extra steps, now use the Physical Flow diagram. It is an unusual characteristic of applying WCB in administration and office or sales environments that it is usually easier to start from the Process analysis tool and progress to the Physical flow tools – the reverse of what we do in manufacturing environments, where the reality of machines and clearly identifiable products makes it easier to see the physical flow.

If we now look at the physical layout of the offices related to the order entry process, we begin to see a picture of wasted movement and time, as in **Figure 23**.

FIGURE 23: ORDER ENTRY PROCESS PAPER FLOW

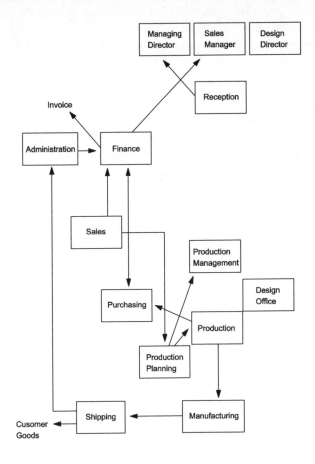

It is immediately clear that there are very many movements involved in entering even a simple order.

If we now look at the time involved in performing this task of order entry, we could look at time in two different ways:

- **Theoretical** - 5 minutes actual time to complete the work involved
- **Actual** - two to three days' elapsed time for all the steps to be completed.

By putting a time/date stamp on an order, or any other piece of paperwork, it is possible to determine the elapsed time or lead-time. In many businesses, lead-times are often very significantly greater than actual processing time. But what can we do to make an improvement?

The answer lies in "What we are trying to do?" Looking at the differences between the theoretical optimum and the actual order entry process, it is clear that much time is lost and energy used by waiting and movement. Paperwork and information must be moved because the skills and experience required to do the work are located separately from each other. Why not bring task-focussed groups of people together from the different functions? Why not have close links between the different departments – in fact, why have the departments at all? If a work group could be formed around the work rather than department heads, then the job could be performed much more easily. True, the job of the manager might be a little more difficult, having to manage distributed staff, but this challenge has been handled in industry for years.

The next two diagrams (**Figures 24** and **25**) show the difference between the traditional and WCB arrangements in an administration setting.

FIGURE 24: ADMINISTRATION - TRADITIONAL

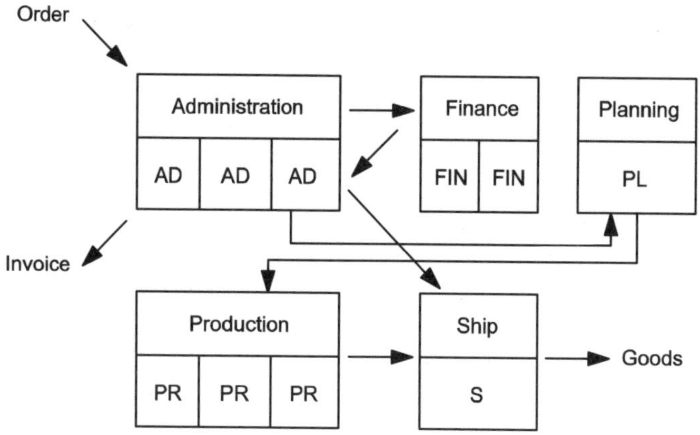

FIGURE 25: ADMINISTRATION –
WORLD CLASS BUSINESS

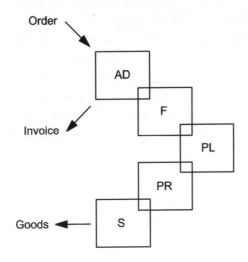

The simple fact of grouping people together, around the task at hand (the process), leads to the opportunity for increased effectiveness and efficiency. People begin to see how they relate to each other, physical movement is reduced significantly and waiting practically disappears. Because all the team members are aware of what is happening in the operation, they are able and ready to support each other and have a peripheral awareness of what jobs are coming at them next. This awareness leads to preparedness and increased operational performance. The office area can, and needs to, provide a business with true world class performance.

But, is this all theory or can it really work in practice? Let's look at two case studies.

Case Study:
International Meat Ingredients

International Meat Ingredients is involved in
the processing of meats to produce value-added meat ingredients for
sale to large restaurant groups and blue-chip food manufacturers. The
company was established in 1993 and employs 65 people

Its main products are salami sausage and meat crumble. Its main
competitors are mainland European companies. Its level of business has
grown dramatically over the past number of years, which has led to
major challenges in structuring the management team and the business
systems to meet the demands of this growth. After achieving ISO
certification without the assistance of an external consultant, the
management team looked for a new challenge and chose WCB as the
tool to focus its development aspirations and to move the company
forward.

Business Process Re-Engineering - Administration

People in the offices had noticed that they were changing from being a
salami factory and becoming a paper factory. Staff were snowed under
with paperwork. They had only part of a system, leading to a multiplicity
of "fixes", with staff creating their own patches to fix inadequacies in the
system. When the team started by mapping the paper trail for a typical
order, this took up a full wall of the board room. The paper trail
consisted of 42 pages, of which 3 were produced by the "system". The
visual impact of the paper trail acted as a key factor to focus
management attention on improving the "system".

The team identified what they considered to be an appropriate system,
and asked the original system supplier to attend a meeting where,
everybody described their requirements. The team used Physical Flow
analysis on the paperwork and re-arranged offices to match the
positioning of people in relation to the process, rather than the process
to the people. The new system now incorporates an inter-departmental
approach to the process of handling administration.

Results Achieved

The key results from this effort are:
- Paperwork reduced by 50%.
- Non-value-added steps reduced.
- Brain-power freed up to find new improvements.

- People now work close beside each other, with their physical location matching the process needs.

Case Study
Tanco Engineering Ltd

The company designs and manufactures a range of agricultural machinery, which is exported to over 20 countries worldwide. Founded in 1963, it is located in Bagnalstown, Co Carlow.

Four days after Liam Lacey bought the company in 1996, planning to develop the business, the first BSE crisis hit the UK market. Senior management decided to focus attention on three key areas of activity under what became known as the "Operations Cost Reduction Programme". This involved:
- Purchasing
- Product Development
- Production.

New product development was seen as a vehicle for moving the business forward, with the Carlow operation supporting these new products from a highly effective operational base.

Development – R&D Team
Focusing initially on the existing products, the team was charged with examining the ranges of options available on machines, with a view to standardising model options and minimising variety. Second, they were charged with examining general specification criteria of competitive products. Third, they were charged with examining, in detail, the specifications of components being used in their machines. Finally, they had to address the issue of manufacturing detail on the current ranges, with a view to simplifying manufacturing processes and removing manufacturing steps where possible.

In parallel with the development of the existing range, the team was also charged with the development of new products and new product concepts, to support the development of the business into the future.

The basic WCB concepts of standardisation, simplification, part-count reduction and inter-departmental teams were applied in the new product development process.

Results Achieved

Tanco managed to remain profitable and to increase productivity and efficiency despite the BSE crisis.

In the design area, the complexity of machines was reduced, leading to easier manufacturing and improved purchasing opportunities. These simpler machines have proven to be more reliable in the field, better performing, easier to manufacture, cheaper to buy components for and cheaper to sell. The design team simultaneously developed new machines for the industrial sector, as well as a world-leading innovative new machine for the agricultural sector.

A result of the WCB activities in Tanco was the development of teams throughout the business. These teams were supportive of each other and continually found ways to improve operational performance by working together. The interaction of people within the business led to the company achieving results that were previously thought – both by staff and external observers – to be beyond its reach.

Future Plans

Tanco's management and staff continue to use and build upon their use of world class practices. It is now looking to develop business opportunities in other sectors, building upon its capabilities in operations, particularly in manufacturing, design and purchasing.

In 2002, Liam Lacey was a finalist in the Ernst & Young Entrepreneur of the Year Awards.

Here, in the Tanco case study, we have sales, finance, purchasing, production planning, production management, stores and design staff all working together, interacting and delivering.

The theory works in reality.

PROCESS & LAYOUT DEVELOPMENT

We have already looked at how to use the Physical Flow and Process Flow analysis tools. But WCB is about continuous improvement, not just making a single improvement and then resting on your laurels. In the next example, we will see how this concept of continuous improvement is made real.

The company under review moulded and assembled electrical components and was under severe pressure to increase output, as demand was high for their products. It was also coming under increasing pressure to reduce costs as they were supplying a major retail chain. It started the improvement process by forming a team and using the Physical Flow and Process Flow analysis tools. The company's original layout and process maps are presented in **Figures 26** and **27**.

FIGURE 26: ASSEMBLY I – PHYSICAL FLOW

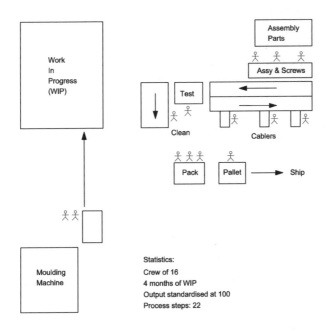

FIGURE 27: ASSEMBLY 1 - PROCESS FLOW

1.	Mould Parts
2.	Pre-assembly 1
3.	Pre-assembly 2
4.	Transfer to WIP
5.	Storage
6.	Transfer to assembly line
7.	Storage
8.	Transfer to Assemblers
9.	Screw
10.	Assemble
11.	Move to conveyor
12.	Sort-cabled/ran cabled
13.	Test
14.	Onto return conveyor
15.	Transfer to cablers
16.	Cable
17.	Onto conveyor
18.	Sort cabled/non cabled
19.	Test
20.	Clean
21.	Pack
22.	Pallet

The team identified movement and high level of WIP as serious issues and developed a new layout, which mainly involved a change in how the process was laid out and in work practices.

When they challenged why the company held four months of stock, the team discovered that there was a concern of not having enough moulded parts to feed the assembly crew. This seemed a logical reason, until analysis showed that the moulding machines were very reliable and that, even if one machine broke down, the company had the resources either to get it going again in a matter of hours or to transfer the mould to another similar machine in the factory. The team decided to reduce the level of WIP stock holding from four months' worth to one months' worth initially, with a future target of one week's worth.

They also decided to relocate the assembly area beside the moulding machine and to re-organise the process. The revised layout and process are presented in **Figures 28** and **29**.

FIGURE 28: ASSEMBLY 2 – PHYSICAL FLOW

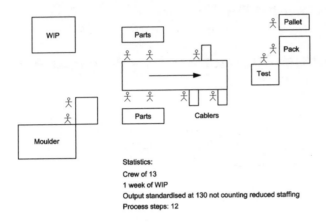

Statistics:
Crew of 13
1 week of WIP
Output standardised at 130 not counting reduced staffing
Process steps: 12

FIGURE 29: ASSEMBLY 2 – PROCESS FLOW

Mould Parts
Pre-Assembly 1
Pre-Assembly 2
Transfer to Storage
Transfer to Conveyor
Screw
Assemble
To Cablers
Cable
Test
Pack
Pallet

The company ran with this process for a number of months, before deciding to re-analyse the process. Having become aware of a newly developed method for joining plastic elements, they moved to detail design the product to:

- Use the new joining method
- Reduce the amount of material used in the product.

Both goals were achieved. The third stage of process development is presented in **Figures 30** and **31**.

FIGURE 30: ASSEMBLY 3 – PHYSICAL FLOW

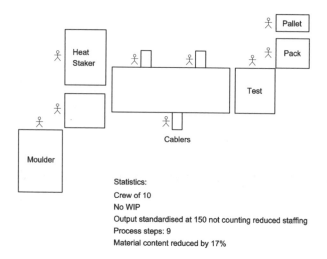

Statistics:
Crew of 10
No WIP
Output standardised at 150 not counting reduced staffing
Process steps: 9
Material content reduced by 17%

FIGURE 31: ASSEMBLY 3 - PROCESS FLOW

Mould Parts
Pre-Assembly 1
Pre-Assembly 2
Heat Staker
Transfer to Conveyor
Cablers
Test
Pack
Pallet

It is still possible to improve this process further. There are still wastes included in the process. More detailed analysis could yield additional savings and improvements, but the example illustrates the continuous improvement approach of looking for more performance from processes by improving them. Improved processes should be challenged after they have settled down, to see whether further improvements can be secured. The hunt for improvement should be on-going.

9: PRODUCTION CONTROL SYSTEMS

Three basic forms of production control system are used in companies employing World Class practices:

- Make to Order
- Kanban
- Rate-based Scheduling.

The type of production system chosen for any given product is usually selected, based on the history of manufacture of the product and its likely future (see **Figure 32**).

FIGURE 32: PRODUCTION SYSTEMS

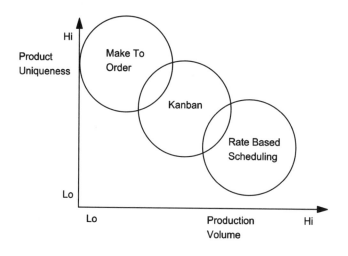

MAKE TO ORDER

If the product is fairly unique or is required in low volumes, then a Make to Order (MTO) approach is probably appropriate.

As the name suggests, product is manufactured only when an order is received. Very little, if any, stock of finished goods is held, because they could be obsolete or have the wrong configuration by the time a customer places an order.

Careful design of products can mean that components and sub-assemblies can be common across a range, enabling the company to produce MTO finished goods relatively quickly. Two very different examples of this approach are used by General Motors (GM) in the USA and Sharp Calculators in Japan. GM uses standardised engines, transmissions and axles across their vehicle ranges, using the bodies and internal fittings to distinguish models. Sharp produces several hundred types of calculator, based on a small number of calculator chips. Features are enabled on the high-end calculators and left dormant on the lower-end ones.

The MTO system is the ultimate goal of all world class operations. Why would a business want to target anything less? In an MTO business, stocks are at a minimum, response time is very short and flexibility is high. The real art in a MTO system is to be able to achieve the benefits of mass production (Rate-based Scheduling) while providing the customer with the option of mass customisation.

The computer industry offers a clear example of how different strategic decisions can impact on a business and its customers and suppliers. Dell Corporation makes computers to order, configuring PCs to meet customers' specific needs. It does not make PCs for stock. Dell has spent a lot of time and effort on developing its core product and a core of suppliers. Dell mass-customises from a relatively restricted palette. In contrast, other computer manufacturers tend to have stocking issues, sometimes having up to 12 weeks' worth of PCs, unsold, in storage. With the speed of change in the PC business, this stock rapidly becomes obsolete. When PCs are made for stock, based on forecasts, the forecasts need be only slightly inaccurate to leave the manufacturer with a serious stock problem.

KanBan

The Kanban or two-bin system is suited to medium-volume, medium-diversity products.

The system is very simple to implement. An estimate of the required output is made, usually based on history and forecasts. This volume then defines the size of the Kanban or bin. If the volume to be produced is chosen as half a week's supply, then two bins are prepared, each capable of holding half a week's production. Product is drawn from the first bin until it is empty, at which time the second bin is accessed and the empty bin is replenished.

The bin can be replenished from the stores, a manufacturing area or by the supplier. The arrival of the empty bin is the trigger for replenishment. There is no checking necessary to count balance stocks or to check stores. As the operation of the system becomes ingrained in the business, and suppliers become more assured with the process of replenishment, it is possible to reduce the stock held in each bin.

Note that the term bin is used loosely: "bins" can be bins, drums, pallets, bags or even silos depending on the material itself.

Looking back at the Dell example, disc drives or computer monitors being managed using a Kanban system.

Case Study:
Burnside Autocyl Ltd

Burnside is an engineering company involved in the production of hydraulic cylinders, primarily for the automotive sector. The main customer base is in Germany. The company has been in existence for 25 years.

In its WCB process, as well as focusing on cells, Burnside also used Kanban techniques quite extensively, in an effort to manage stocks and suppliers in an effective and efficient way. Subcontractors can now bring in materials and stock them directly into the stores.

A trolley system was introduced for holding Kanban quantities of parts, allowing flexibility of moving heavy parts and large numbers of parts around the factory. This tidied up the cells and meant that workers did not have to wait for a fork-lift truck to come to service the cell.

Materials, equipment and consumables are now located at the work areas, under the control of the team leaders, who monitor their own local stocks and requisition materials as they needed them. This means that workers do not have to go to the Stores during the day to ask for drills, tools or other pieces. In turn, the Stores staff do not have to "man the hatch", or to interrupt their stores and materials-related work to service petty requests. This freeing up of Stores staff time led to increased supplier development and increased levels of availability of materials in the plant.

Results Achieved
After the implementation of the WCB programme:
- Raw material stocks were reduced by 50%
- Stocks were booked to each cell, reducing WIP by 25%
- Stock turnover was up from 3 times a year to 5
- Consumable stores were replaced with a flexible pallet and trolley system.

Rate-based Scheduling
The Rate-based Scheduling (RBS) approach is best suited to mature products with secure positions in the market, where history and forecasts indicate that market demand is steady and the products lend themselves to mass production or dedicated process-type manufacture.

Under RBS, production time, staff and resources are allocated based on rolling forecasts, and materials are ordered under long-term arrangements with suppliers. The food industry is a good example of the application of RBS. Products such as jams, ketchups, bread, cereals, etc. are manufactured using RBS.

As production volumes increase, there is an opportunity to move towards more dedicated, automated machinery, where the effort required to automate processes can be recouped over the life of the product.

Note that the type of production system best suited to the manufacture of a given product can, and often will, change over the life cycle of the product (see **Figure 33**).

FIGURE 33: LIFE CYCLE & CHOICE OF MANUFACTURING SYSTEMS

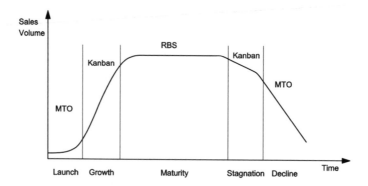

10: Saving Time

As seen earlier, time is critical in both manufacturing and office/sales environment. Let's look at some more WCB tools that help to save time.

The Shadow Board

The most costly tool in any manufacturing operation is the one that cannot be found when needed! The time lost in production due to missing tools or parts can often greatly outweigh the cost of the tools themselves.

The Shadow Board was developed to help address the issue of missing or mis-laid tools. A board is erected in the required area, with the outline of tools or an identification mark inscribed on the board. If the tool is missing, it is clear to see and also easy to know which one is missing. **Figure 34** shows of two ways of keeping tools in a manufacturing area.

FIGURE 34: TOOLBOX vs SHADOW BOARD

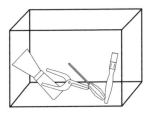

Toolbox

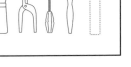

Shadow Board

What tool is missing from the toolbox?
What tool is missing from the shadow board?
Which way of keeping tools would you prefer to rely on?

The simple fact of having defined locations for tools and equipment can help to reduce lost time spent looking for missing items.

EARLY WARNING SYSTEMS

Much of what we have talked about so far, such as check sheets and run charts, tell us about what has happened in the past. We now look at WCB techniques that will tell us about the future, giving early warnings of problems that could lead to failures, rejects or lost production.

Many of today's machines are fitted with early warning systems, sensors and annunciators – lights or buzzers, which advise an operator if a machine:

- Is operating satisfactorily
- Is about to run out of materials or about to shut down
- Has stopped.

This combination of sensors, lights and buzzers can give operators sufficient notice to avoid machine jams or stoppages. Because the system is so simple, it is very easy to retrofit to older machines and processors. With early warning systems fitted, it often becomes possible for an operator to run several machines at a time, servicing the needs of individual machines as required as opposed to being stuck at a single machine watching it work. Carefully arranging machines can help the operator to do this task.

The early warning systems are frequently found on the supply systems to automated machines. A typical example of this is on the decoiling and straightening system for a press machine, shown in **Figure 35**. The sensors and lights can warn the operator when a coil is about to run out, allowing them time to prepare the next coil for feeding into the machine, avoiding a jam as the tail end of the coil moves through the press. The system can also warn of the completion of a batch, alerting the operator to the need to remove product and change-over to the next job. In addition, the system can alert the operator to a machine stoppage, calling them to free the machine and restart manufacture.

FIGURE 35: EARLY WARNING SYSTEMS 1 - LIGHT

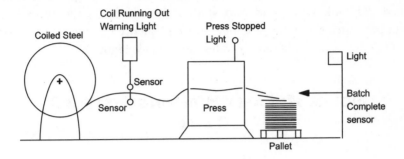

The key objective of using these early warning devices is to free staff to do other, more value-adding (and usually, more interesting) work.

An example of level controls and warning lights shown in a previous book of the authors was adapted recently for an industrial application. The example showed a hopper, as in **Figure 36**, with a level gauge and a warning light to warn the operator when the level had gone low.

FIGURE 36: EARLY WARNING SYSTEMS 2 - HOPPER

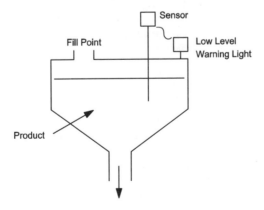

This was a system that one of the authors developed when working with Nestlé, on a semi-automated system he built to make Chef Mayonnaise!

The hopper was used to supply lubricating fluid to a perforating press. Prior to its installation, an operator spent his working day standing beside the press, "watching" the machine and topping up the small perforating fluid reservoir. Then the company built a 7-gallon steel tank and mounted it on the side of the press. Each morning, the operator filled the tank with fluid and started the press. As the fluid level dropped during the day, the operator had plenty of time to add more fluid to the reservoir before the tank ran dry (see **Figure 37**).

FIGURE 37: EARLY WARNING SYSTEMS 3 - TANK

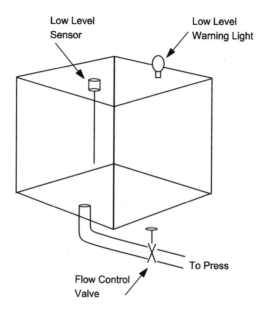

The company moved a second rolling press close to the perforating press, as the output of the perforating press was used to feed the rolling press. This move meant that one operator could run both presses, that the physical movement of coils was minimised and performance was increased. The layout before, and after, this work is presented in **Figures 38** and **39**.

FIGURE 38: COILER - BEFORE

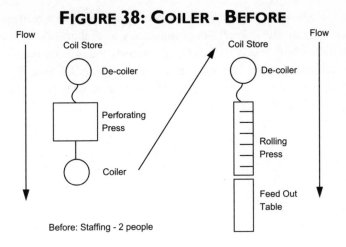

Before: Staffing - 2 people

FIGURE 39: COILER – AFTER

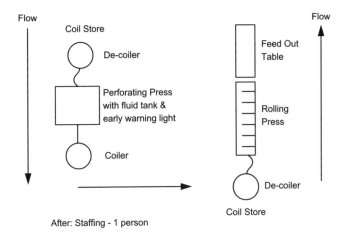

After: Staffing - 1 person

Mark Your Gauges!

Another simple technique to help ensure that plant and machinery operate correctly is to mark gauges.

Fuel, temperature, or oil gauges in a car indicate clearly what areas are good and what areas are bad – red is usually a sign of a danger zone. We can apply a similar approach to industrial machines. If gauges are marked, the operator can see immediately whether the needles are pointing to the right zone. If there are multiple gauges in a control panel, why not align all the correct operating zones so that an operator can see immediately whether any dial indicates outside the normal range.

The same approach can be applied to machine settings. By noting settings on the machine in the relevant positions, operators and fitters can know what settings need to be.

11: MAINTENANCE

Machines break down. To prevent this, they need to be maintained. If they break down when they are needed for production, this can cause real problems. Maintenance, when correctly used, can improve the overall performance of a plant.

Much maintenance activity is based on the understanding of machine life cycles, represented in **Figure 40**.

FIGURE 40: PROBABILITY OF FAILURE

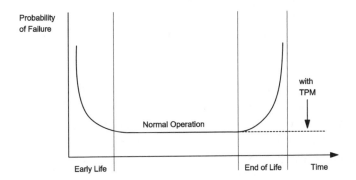

Engineers have identified that machines have a particular life cycle. The early days of their working lives are likely to give rise to teething problems. Once a machine has passed through this phase, it tends to work normally for a long period but, as it approaches the end of its working life, it tends to give problems again.

THE BASICS OF MAINTENANCE

Maintenance makes an effort to prolong the period of normal operation. This is achieved by using action teams, focused on the machine, the area and their issues, using the core WCB tools already presented.

The basics of good maintenance can be described quite simply:

- Machines and work areas need to be clean and free of clutter.
- Work areas need to be organised.
- Operators need to care for their machines.
- Operators need to understand the process.
- Operators should do basic checks on the machines.
- Operators should do basic maintenance on the machines.

Cleaning

By cleaning their machines and their working area, the operators develop a sense of ownership for their environment. This mundane task also gives the operator a chance to get to know their equipment better and to be able to identify problems as they develop. As the operator becomes more experienced, they will build on their ability to predict failures and problems before these become sources of loss for the business.

A clean workplace is generally a better and nicer environment to work in. A clean work area is also generally a safer work area. If clutter is removed, and spills of lubricant and material are cleaned up or prevented, then trip hazards are minimised. It seems obvious, but good housekeeping can help a great deal in presenting your business well and in building the morale of people throughout the organisation.

Organising

The old adage "Everything in its place and a place for everything" is a very appropriate one. Time spent looking for a missing tool or part is often time that could have been spent more productively.

There should be specific locations defined for materials, finished goods and tools. Machine-specific tools should be located beside the machine, preferably on a Shadow Board.

Kanban squares for materials and finished goods can help ensure that sufficient materials are available for production but not too much.

An organised work area is more effective and efficient than a disorganised one.

Caring

Operators need to care for their machines, their work areas and their work. Managers need to care about their processes.

It may seem strange to use "care" in an industrial sense, but it is a valid use of the word. Unless we care about what we are doing, we are being "careless" with our work.

If a machine stops, people need to care enough to get it going again, quickly and correctly. People need to care enough about what they are doing to want to work to improve performance, to want to use the WCB tools to identify root causes of problems.

Understanding

Operators need to be trained to understand their machines, their processes and the impact of changes they might make. People often *think* they know what they are doing and managers can easily *assume* that operators understand the detailed impact of their actions. But this is often not true. It is not enough that the chief engineer, supervisor or fitters understand the process, businesses that want to be world class must work to the point where all key staff know and understand the processes they work with.

TYPES OF MAINTENANCE

We first considered maintenance at Level 1, when we looked at Fixed Time Maintenance (**Chapter 5**). Now we look at the other types of maintenance, including:

- Condition-based maintenance
- Opportunity maintenance
- Operation to failure
- Design out maintenance.

Condition-based Maintenance

By monitoring changes in plant and equipment, it is possible to notice deterioration and plan a response before failure occurs.

Many of the actions used to implement condition-based maintenance (CBM) are simple:

- Wiping a surface
- Listening to a machine
- Smelling for heat build-up
- Looking at a machine action or a shaft's rotation
- Feeling for vibrations
- Testing fluids or product.

Obviously, care needs to be taken when using these techniques to avoid injury but they can be very effective in the early diagnosis of developing machine problems. Operators can develop a very heightened sense of their machines and can often detect a deteriorating condition before the machine fails. They may not always be able to describe technically what is going wrong but they can often help the fitter or engineer to home in on the issue.

Current developments in technology have made available a wide range of advanced equipment to maintenance staff, which can accurately measure vibration, heat, concentricity and many other characteristics of plant and equipment. Many of the benefits of this equipment can be achieved through the use of the five human senses.

Opportunity Maintenance

Under an opportunity maintenance programme, partially-worn parts are replaced when other parts require attention under a time-based or condition-based maintenance programme. While these parts may not be fully worn-out, the cost of stopping the machine a second time to replace them when they do eventually wear out, usually far outweighs the cost of the parts themselves. So the cost-effective decision is often to replace a number of parts at the same time, following the failure of a single part. The final decision as to what parts are changed is based on experience and a thorough examination during the strip-down.

Operation to Failure

As the name implies, this not really a maintenance strategy at all but more of a "non-maintenance" strategy. If machines or components can be easily replaced with minimal disruption, then they can be run until they break, when they can be replaced. By standardising on key equipment, it may be possible to have spare units available to replace failed ones.

In the food industry, for example, pumps are often run in harsh environments. By standardising on the size and shape of pump stand, fittings and the electrical plug and socket connections, a business can run a pump until it fails and then replace the complete pump unit in minutes, ensuring availability of the full system.

Design Out Maintenance

The cheapest maintenance to do is the maintenance that does not need to be done. If machines are designed not to need maintenance, while providing reliable service, then this can be a source of saving. The sealed battery in motor cars is a classic example of maintenance that has been designed out.

12: Practical Quality

Quality is a universal concern for all businesses and organisations. It is equally important for public bodies that provide services to companies and individuals, as it is for private sector companies.

An understanding of quality and quality tools is essential to build competitiveness into the future. Customers and clients will not accept the levels of quality that were acceptable even 10 years ago. The old attitude of "It will be good enough!" must be destroyed and replaced with one where products and services are of the highest quality, and worth the asking price.

Ireland has been a world leader in the adoption of the ISO 9000 quality standard. This has had both a positive and a negative effect on Irish business. On the positive side, the adoption of the standard has meant that the business takes quality seriously and has appointed a quality champion or representative. On the negative side, many people seemed to think that, once an ISO 9000 system was in place, "Quality" was taken care of. If there is a "Quality Department", surely quality is their responsibility. However, **"Quality is Everybody's Responsibility!"**

Quality cannot be added after the fact. No amount of measuring, testing, counting or evaluating will add quality to a service or product. Quality can only be added to a service or product during the value-adding parts of the process.

Consider a typical service organisation, say a bank. If the bank is cluttered, disorganised and badly-run with bad mannered staff or overly complicated systems, we will think poorly of the place and wonder whether our money is better elsewhere. Restaurant customers who find the toilets dirty or badly taken care of can only hope the kitchens are better managed and more hygienic. In a manufacturing environment, if the product is badly designed, poor quality materials bought and the product badly made with little care and attention, then the best quality department on the island can add no quality to the delivered product.

People throughout the business need to understand that they are an integral part of this quality chain and not separate from it.

This shared awareness of quality and how employees are a part of, and integrated into, the chain needs to be introduced to all employees by a committed and dedicated management. True business excellence and customer care are at the heart of this approach. Training of management and staff becomes an essential part of getting this message across, until it becomes the natural way of life within the business.

The approach could be called Quality Function Deployment for small and medium-sized companies. By deploying quality throughout the business, by making everyone responsible for their own contribution to quality, real levels of improvement can be achieved. The approach is akin to expecting that all employees act with skill and dedication – like craftsmen of old. People need to care about what they do if they are to have respect for themselves, their output and the business.

But how do we translate these high ideals into practical reality? There are many books written on the detail of quality systems. For a very deep understanding of the theory of quality, these texts should be studied. If a practical move to improve operational performance is required, there is a core of tools that can help do this, easily. We have already been introduced to the core WCB tools of Physical Flow and Process Flow analysis, check sheets and run charts, all supported by the use of teams. Now we will look at some further, relatively simple, quality tools and techniques that can help to identify the root sources of waste in an operation and to address them. Some of these tools are universal, while others are more specifically associated with manufacturing businesses. We will deal with the universal tools first.

WCB OR ISO – WHICH COMES FIRST?

The question is often asked, which comes first, the ISO quality standard or a WCB initiative? The answer is that it depends. The new version of ISO 9000 now includes continuous improvement as an integral part of the quality system. The new system even says that businesses should benchmark themselves. Now the distance between ISO and WCB has closed.

By taking the WCB route, a business will strengthen the abilities and capabilities of its staff, while developing and improving its processes and performance. By following the ABC route outlined in this book, including objective benchmarking against international sectoral performance and practice models, a business will truly be working towards developing its capabilities. When this basic work of improving and developing internal performance is completed, it should be a relatively simple matter to create procedures for the processes, and to write the manual to ISO standards.

If, on the other hand, the time and resources are available from the beginning to follow the ISO implementation route, then the business will undoubtedly succeed in writing procedures to describe their processes and, in time, will improve those processes when it adopts continuous improvement and benchmarking techniques.

Both routes will lead to a similar goal, although the ABC route is most likely to get there earlier and with a more company-wide team-based approach. The ABC organisation will have built the capability of its people in improving systems and processes and in working together. The ISO organisation will be very good at writing procedures and building a quality manual. You pay your money and take your choice!

CUSTOMER COMPLAINTS
AS A DATA SOURCE

All businesses have customers or clients, whether they be public or private enterprises, service or manufacturing operations, profit or non-profit. The fact that customers or clients exist usually means that there will be a high degree of customer satisfaction, but equally it means that there will often be some level of customer dissatisfaction or complaint.

Customer complaints are a very rich source of opportunity to improve processes. However, it is important to realise that not all customer complaints are valid or true. This is often a delicate issue, but needs to be recognised and managed. If a business or organisation accepts a totally customer-biased response to complaints, then it is open to abuse by a small percentage of its clients.

That said, the first question a business or organisation needs to ask itself is: "Are records available of all complaints received?". If there is no system to capture complaints received, then it is unlikely that complaints will be captured, and even more unlikely that they will be analysed and less unlikely again that the business will benefit from the potential to improve its processes that such complaints could deliver to the business.

A system to capture customer complaints can be as simple as a file to store written complaints and a simple form to capture telephoned or spoken complaints.

Use a check sheet to analyse the complaints. Many companies often deal with individual complaints as just that – individual complaints. They fail to analyse complaints over time, and thus miss trends, or seasonal factors, or hot spots in their processes that contribute to complaints.

An action team should be formed to analyse and discuss the complaints in an effort to devise a company-wide response to the issues identified by the analysis. Often complaints are handled by sales or quality department staff, without recourse to those sections of the business that are responsible for the source of the problem.

Then use a run chart to record:

- The overall level of customer complaints
- The causes of complaints.

The run chart gives the business the opportunity to monitor progress over time and to work to reduce the overall incidence of complaints.

A customer complaints team that is representative of all elements of the operation can lead to a highly focused and successful initiative across the business.

THE MEASLES DIAGRAM

Much modern machinery and plant is complex and often of quite a large scale. The measles diagram helps to identify areas of such machinery that cause problems. It is an evolution from the check sheet where, rather than working with a list of problems that may occur in a process, a pictogram of the machine or process is developed. Each time a problem occurs in a particular part of the machine or plant, the operator puts a dot – a measle – on the pictogram (see **Figure 41**).

The level of detail of the pictogram depends on an estimate of where problems are occurring. If more detail is needed, it is often better to draw detailed sketches of specific parts of a machine and leave them located around the machine rather than developing one big sketch for the whole machine.

FIGURE 41: MEASLES DIAGRAM

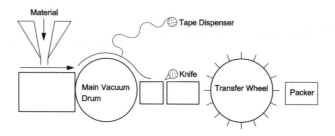

The second iteration of this sketch could use detailed sketches at both the "Knife" and "Tape Dispenser" areas to capture further detail on the specific issues arising in those areas.

HISTOGRAMS

Histograms allow us to "see" data using a graphical approach.

Information is gathered from the process and represented using a bar graph. The histogram is usually used to represent frequency of occurrence of data. It can be used successfully to record such diverse data sets as sales of trucks by model, to thickness of machined parts to numbers of faults or complaints recorded by department.

The use of the histogram in a sales environment can be greatly enhanced by the introduction of a target line. In the following example, the sales of different models of trucks are used to show how the histogram can be used (**Figure 42**).

FIGURE 42: SALES OF TRUCKS - DATA

Week No.	10				
Model	"45"	"75"	"95"	"6 X 4"	"8 X 4"
Number Sold	3	7	3	2	3

The data is usually captured daily or weekly to give managers an insight into the trends at play. The data is then entered onto the histogram.

FIGURE 43: SALES OF TRUCKS - HISTOGRAM

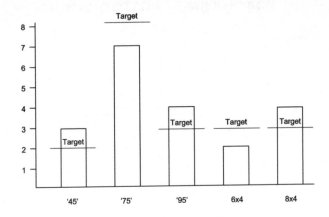

Once again, the inclusion of the target line on the histogram for sales can be helpful as both a challenge, and a recognition, of achievement.

The more usual use of the histogram is in manufacturing, where it can be used to check variation in a process. In this next example, the length of parts after a machining process is measured, as in **Figure 44**.

FIGURE 44: LENGTH OF PARTS AFTER MACHINING - DATA

Length	7.1	7.2	7.3	7.4	7.5
Frequency	5	10	27	13	3

Now the histogram is developed further to help the user to see the data, as in **Figure 45**.

FIGURE 45: LENGTH OF PARTS AFTER MACHINING - HISTOGRAM

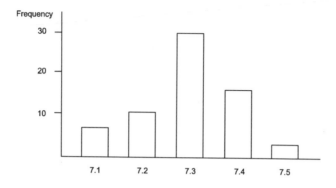

If the specification for length of parts was set at 7.1 to 7.3, we can see from the histogram that the process is tending to make parts too long, and is even producing parts outside the specification. The histogram can be helpful in seeing these results and initiating action to resolve them.

CONTROLLING PROCESSES

The control of processes is essential to delivering quality services or products to the customers. A number of techniques have been developed to help management gain, and retain, confidence that procedures will be followed and quality standards maintained.

Starting Up

Before a process can be "released to customers", it needs to be started. For example, airline pilots work through extensive checklists before taking to the air. In a more mundane business, think of a fast-food outlet where controls and checklists are in place to ensure refrigeration, cooking and maintenance temperatures are correct before the first meals of the day are served.

In a front-office business, are all the correct forms and documents in place, and in sufficient quantities, before opening for business? In a retail outlet, have shelves been restocked, are bags available in place, are sufficient till rolls in place and is the shop tidy?

Most business can benefit from having a "pre-opening" or pre-starting business checklist to ensure that all relevant items are present and correct.

Pre-production Control Sheet

In a manufacturing business, the checks are often more specific. Parts and components are generally manufactured to a specification, which must be met.

A pre-production quality check will often include such details as checking that the correct tooling is being used, that the correct materials are available and that key dimensional tolerances are being achieved. An example of a pre-production control sheet is presented in **Figure 46**.

FIGURE 46: PRE-PRODUCTION CONTROL SHEET

Operator: _____

Date: _____ **Shift:** _____

Tool Number: Description:

Sample No.	Width	Height	Length
1			
2			
3			

Checked: _____

Clear to Run: _____

The availability of simple-to-use, and relatively cheap, digital instruments has made it an easy task for most operators to use precision instruments, such as verniers and micrometers, with minimal training. This can bring major benefits, in terms of ultimate product quality at low cost.

Running Your Process

Once the process is started correctly, it is important to keep it running and to be sure that it is running at the quality levels set. Since the manager cannot be present all the time to ensure this, In Process Inspection (IPI) has been developed as a means of ensuring quality levels are maintained. Examples of IPI include public conveniences, where a control sheet shows who last performed a check on cleanliness – and when. In major food outlets, regular checks are made on the temperature of chilled food cabinets. In power generation stations, regular checks are made on the status of many parameters to ensure that the plant is running both efficiently and well.

Run charts can record IPI data and monitor the process. An example of a run chart is presented in **Figure 47**.

FIGURE 47: RUN CHART

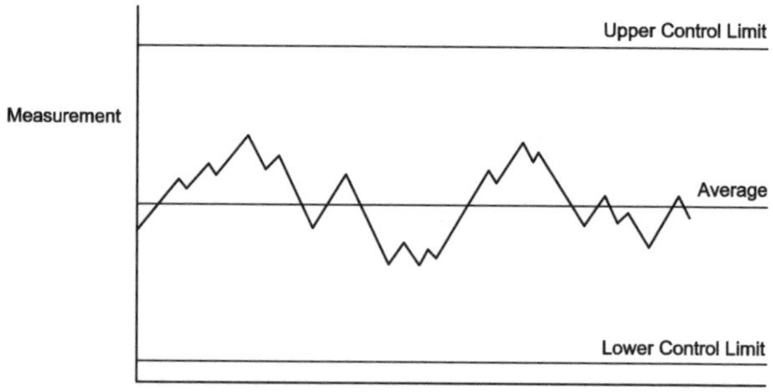

Case Study: Medentech Ltd

Medentech was formed in 1984 and is a leading player in the disinfection and water purification fields worldwide. It develops and manufactures effervescent tablets for use in human and animal hygiene sectors. The company employs 50 people.

Run Charts
The company used Run Charts extensively in its tableting and packaging areas. The charts helped management and staff to monitor effectiveness of processes and also to capture and show improvements made. Staff were able to see graphically the results of their efforts to improve processes. This helped to motivate them to tackle more challenging issues.

Sampling Your Process

The process has been started and the normal checks and controls are in place, but are management really getting a full and accurate view?

In a service business, blind testing provides the opportunity of seeing what the customer perceives. This can be done by telephoning the business or by getting a friend or specialist analysis company to obtain service from the business, to see just what the experience is like for customers or clients.

In a manufacturing business, the question of what to measure can often be a difficult one. Normal in-process inspection can only measure two to three attributes. However, most parts, components or products have many more attributes. The sample analysis report facilitates this process. By restricting the process to a small sample of parts, it becomes possible to check and measure many more attributes than during the normal in-process inspection. An example of the sample analysis report is presented in **Figure 48**.

FIGURE 48: SAMPLE ANALYSIS REPORT

Product: _____

Date: _____   **Person:** _____

	Sample				
	1	2	3	4	5
Height					
Length					
Width					
Thickness					
Weight					
Shape					
Colour					

SCRAP/REJECT REPORTS

The waste bin is an invaluable source of information for management and staff focussed on an improvement initiative. Since the bin contains waste, careful analysis may provide insights into the causes of defects and scrap. The breakdown of rejects into internally-generated or supplier-related can help focus attention on the relevant area. An example of a scrap/reject report is presented in **Figure 49**.

FIGURE 49: SCRAP/REJECT REPORT

Person: _____ **Date:** _____

Reject No.	Description	Fault	Disposition
407	End Pin	No screw	Hold - supplier
408	Cross Bar	Bent	Rework - internal
409	Cross Stop	Scratched	Scrap - internal

The scrap/reject report can provide a basis for feedback to suppliers. By quantifying objectively the source of faults, factual information to discuss with your suppliers is gained.

OUTPUT REPORTS

Output reports are most frequently used in the manufacturing arena. They provide management with the opportunity to capture information, typically from individual machines. The output reports can be relatively simple, as in **Figure 50**.

FIGURE 50: OUTPUT REPORT I

Day:
Shift:
Output:

All the information that the manager gets will be the overall output for the shift. This information could be charted, using a run chart, to see if it varies over time. However, the information is quite limited.

Developing the report a stage further, one could look for records of the amount of downtime being incurred during a shift. This could lead to a report as in **Figure 51**.

FIGURE 51: OUTPUT REPORT 2

Day:
Shift:
Output:
Downtime:

The manager and operator now both have a view of trends over time and can begin to discuss improvement initiatives to address downtime.

The next evolution of the output report provides further information to manager and operator and can be very helpful in identifying issues, as in **Figure 52**.

FIGURE 52: OUTPUT REPORT 3

	Hour							
	1	2	3	4	5	6	7	8
Day:								
Shift:								
Output:								
Downtime:								

This level of detail lends itself to further analysis, with the run chart format being particularly suited to this work. As an example, **Figure 53** presents the data from a typical process over an eight-hour working day.

FIGURE 53: OUTPUT CHART

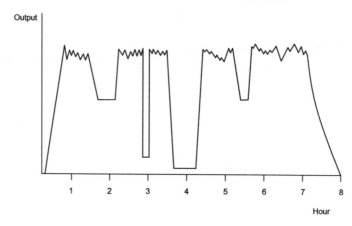

Examining this run chart may identify issues that may have been neglected or missed over time, as in **Figure 54**.

FIGURE 54: OUTPUT CHART ANNOTATED

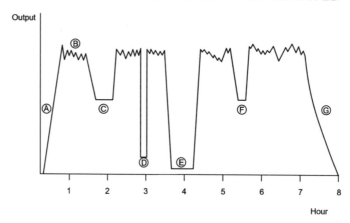

The issues include:

    A. **Start up losses** – Time can be lost first thing in the morning, getting materials organised and machines started. Could this waste be reduced by employing a "start-up person" who comes in early to prepare rather than losing the output of the full work force?

B. "Normal" disruptions, usually adjustments and tweaks, small jams and interruptions. These can often be difficult to address but can be very fertile ground for improvement team activities.

C. Coffee break – half the operators at a time, meaning a reduction in production output.

D. Machine breakdown – requires an input from maintenance to get the process running again.

E. Lunch break

F. Afternoon tea!

G. Closing down losses, as people get ready to go home, they begin to wind down and clean up. Could a specialist cleaning crew be employed to tackle this work, ensuring full production until the end of the day?

But there is one loss that is not shown on this run chart that is often missed: the difference between design output levels and normal operating levels, as shown in **Figure 55**. Often we tend to run machines below their design levels due to poor materials, maintenance or adjustment. We should really try to run machines and processes at their design speeds and even beyond, by fixing the issues that normally prevent us from doing this.

FIGURE 55: OUTPUT CHART SHOWING POTENTIAL

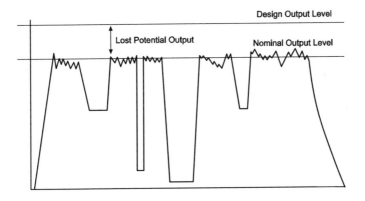

Output reports can also be used in service and retail operations. A "footfall" chart is often used in retail business to get a picture of when customers and potential customers are present. A similar chart can be used to record the timing and level of incoming telephone calls, thereby identifying an optimised pattern of attendance for reception and order-taking staff, ensuring sufficient staff are present when clients require service.

CONTROL CHARTS

We are now moving into the realm of the quality professional. The section on control charts and the section on process capability are most suited to advanced users of quality tools, who are working with a quality expert and specialist quality publications.

The control chart is a development of the run chart, in which, using statistical methods, upper and lower control limits are determined. These limits are calculated using data gathered while the process is operating normally. Any adjustments made should be normal ones rather than remedial ones.

An example of a control chart with control and working limits is shown in **Figure 56.**

FIGURE 56: CONTROL CHART

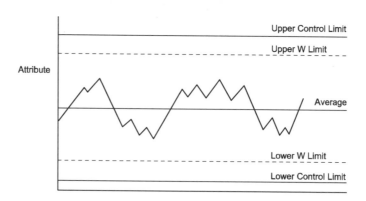

The use of statistical process control (SPC) through control charts can be very useful in a mass production or precision engineering environment.

Statistical process control removes discussion from the realm of opinion firmly into the arena of facts. By improving the process, it becomes possible to reduce the gap between the upper and lower limits and to be assured of manufacturing components to a given measurement.

Be careful, however, when using SPC, to understand what the charts are actually saying. If the process is running between the upper and lower limits, this only means that the process is running *consistently*, it does not necessarily mean that the parts are being produced to the required specification.

A process is said to be in statistical control if a number of criteria are satisfied:

1. No value lies outside the control limits.
2. No more than about one in 40 values lies between the warning and control limits.
3. No examples of two consecutive values lie in the same warning zone.
4. No runs of more than six values lie either side of the average line.
5. No runs of more than six values are all rising or all falling.

With the process under control, we can now turn our attention to determining whether the process can meet the required specification.

PROCESS CAPABILITY

The attention so far has been on processes and how they work in their own right. But processes are put in place to deliver on an objective, to meet a specification.

Where a control chart shows whether a process is under control, a capability chart shows whether the process can consistently meet the specification requirements.

When a business starts to use Process Capability, it needs the input of quality professionals, as this can be a complex area.

13: Teams & Team-Building – Employee Involvement

People are probably the most important resource of an effective organisation. It is through the efforts and creativity of people that customer and client needs are serviced and future innovative responses are developed. People are needed to run and develop office processes, manufacturing and distribution processes and sales processes.

If people are so centrally important to the delivery of service or product to customers, it is clear that they need to be involved in the improvement activities. In a company following the principles of ABC, people are required to *think* as well as *do*. The ABC approach relies upon the active involvement of people in the improvement process, and the team approach is the common means of delivering on this.

People need to be trained in how teams work, and how they can learn to work together to solve problems. The tools and techniques of team-building will be addressed in this chapter, although not all problems require the use of teams – many can be addressed by individuals.

Nonetheless, the real challenge for management today is to harness the full potential of their people, to capture and channel their efforts to achieve the goals and objectives of the business.

Company Culture

The culture of a company or organisation is largely dependent on its leadership. People in a business respond depending on how they perceive the requirements of management. If managers have an open, positive attitude to developing their operations, working with their people to deliver this, the most staff will respond positively. If managers adopt a closed, autocratic style, then staff will respond by taking cover, protecting themselves and generally being unwilling to participate in improvement activities.

Managers decide which style of operation they want to manage. Many managers believe they are the only ones capable of doing the job "right" – the old adage "if you want a job done right then you need to do it yourself" seems to be their motto. If this is true, then the business has a serious problem because even the very best individuals are limited by the amount of hours in the day.

Before deciding which type of business management style to adopt, it can be useful to ask what could be achieved if there were others with the same focus and commitment working in the business? Imagine if, rather than having just one capable, enthusiastic and committed person, there were 10 or 20 or 100, all working for the same goal, all doing their best. The real challenge facing management is to give the others in a business a shared goal, an objective that they can work towards and help deliver. This can be difficult to achieve but the rewards are certainly worthwhile. Remember, the manager, the leader, sets the culture.

The importance of management's role in this area cannot be understated. If the people in a business are to deliver to their true potential then management must create and sustain an environment where staff's contributions are both sought and recognised. Management sets the values by which the business operates. If the values are set high, then staff are likely to aspire to meet them. If the value system of the business is set low, then the business is very likely to meet that low target too.

The question of a business value system underpinned by respect, respect for its people, its customers and society is very well summed up in a phrase often used by Liam Lacey of Tanco Engineering, used to describe the value system of the business, and shown in **Figure 57**.

FIGURE 57: VALUE SYSTEM

Fairness, Firmness, Consistency. Liam Lacey, Tanco Engineering	
Fairness	Everyone is entitled to be treated fairly, a balance needs to be struck between the needs of individuals and the business.
Firmness	When policy has been decided upon and defined, it will be followed.
Consistency	The same rules apply to all.

APPROPRIATE STRUCTURES

The way businesses are structured can have a major impact on how staff respond and how they work.

The traditional approach to business organisation led to specialisation and departmentalisation at management levels, as in **Figure 58**. The accountant took control of the finances, the finance department and the finance staff. The sales manager took control of, and responsibility for, the sales function and the sales and sales support staff. The manufacturing manager, likewise, took control of manufacturing and all that entails. This departmentalised approach leads to the creation of a typical organisation chart.

FIGURE 58: ORGANISATION STRUCTURE

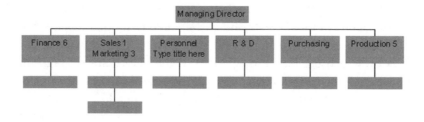

People are placed within the organisation according to their expertise and experience. The financial matters are handled by, and in, the finance department; the same is true of each of the other departments. This approach can be effective and efficient, if all the work to be done by a department is under the control of the department. However, this is often not the case.

How many customers needs are addressed by any one department in a business? Let's take a simple example to illustrate this point, where a customer wants to place an order for a standard product, as in **Figure 59**.

FIGURE 59: PLACING AN ORDER

1. The sales person visits the customer and receives the order. The completed order docket is brought back to the office and handed to the order entry clerk.
2. The order entry clerk enters the order in the "system" and delivers the daily sales report to the sales manager.
3. The next day the daily sales sheets are transferred to Warehousing.
4. Warehousing has four of the five items ordered in stock, so they place an order to Production for the out-of-stock item.
5. Warehousing then prepare the other four items for shipping and send the paperwork to Finance for invoicing.
6. Production ask Purchasing to obtain raw materials and plan to manufacture the items.

Meanwhile, Finance informs Warehousing that the customer is on hold due to an outstanding bill and advises them not to ship the four items they have already picked. Warehousing tells Sales, and so it goes on.

Each of these inter-departmental communications takes time and leads to delays in meeting customer needs.

The same process map can be carried out for each of the many customer-related and supplier-related interactions within a business. The resulting Physical Flow and Process Flow maps will help identify wastes.

Arranging the structure of the business differently, along process rather than departmental lines, might remove significant delays and wastes. A revised structure is presented in **Figure 60**.

Staff are allocated to areas of the business according to business need. Finance staff are located in the sales and purchasing areas, and thus they can identify quickly which customers may cause problems and can make sure that key suppliers are paid on time, ensuring availability of materials. The departmental heads are still in place, ensuring a professional approach is maintained and that the management team retain a coherent approach to managing the business. This process-oriented structure removes many wastes from the operation and helps build understanding and team work within the business.

FIGURE 60: ORGANISATION STRUCTURE - REVISED

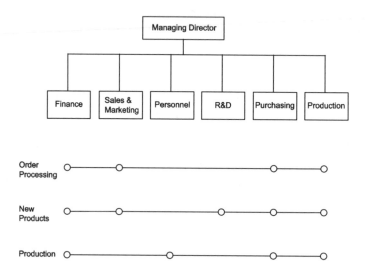

TEAM-BUILDING

We have already looked at the four stages of team-building:

- Forming
- Storming
- Norming
- Performing.

We will now look at the more practical aspects of how teams are built. There are a number of basic steps to be followed when forming teams the most obvious of these steps is deciding whether a team is required to achieve the result. Not all tasks need a team to address them. Some tasks are better handled by individuals, focused to achieve results. However, once it has been decided that the scale of the task needs a team to solve it, the process of team building can begin.

Team Selection

Teams are formed to solve problems or develop processes, because of the benefits of having more than one brain working on the problem. It is important that the chosen team members bring something of value to the team. Their knowledge, skills and experience should be relevant to the task facing the team. There is usually very little point in having a machine operator join a team focused on developing the sales process. By the same token, if the team is focused on addressing problems with customer complaints, then the team should have representatives from sales, production, quality and finance, to ensure that the full response of the company is brought to bear on such a wide-ranging issue.

Many small and medium-sized companies are often restricted in their choices when it comes to team selection, since they have only a small pool of people to draw from. This can lead to some difficulties, especially where personalities can be a problem.

Team Leadership

Effective team leadership is critical. The leader needs to find ways to build on the strengths and abilities of the team members in an effort to achieve the goals and objectives of the team, and the business. The team leader needs to know about and understand the basic WCB tools and techniques and needs to be able to transfer this understanding to the team members. The leader needs to be familiar with brainstorming, be capable of negotiating, and be able to deal with inter-personal issues. The leader needs to be driven to achieve the goals of the team and also able to lead and drive the team as circumstances demand.

Positive interaction between team members is critical to the success of a team. The leader needs to try and create an environment where creativity of team members can flourish and where ideas and innovations are developed and worked to the point that they contribute to achieving the overall team objectives. The leader needs to ensure that all team members contribute to the task at hand. The leader needs to be sensitive to the personalities in the team, to ensure the vibrant personalities do not drown out the quieter ones. The team needs to learn the art of active listening, realising that some people do not like to take a leading role but that they very often have something positive to contribute.

The leader needs to ensure that the team bases its decisions on facts rather than opinions. The basic quality tools of check sheets and run charts can be helpful in this regard. And finally, the leader needs to help the team develop to the point where it takes responsibility for its own actions. The team needs to be strong enough to accept challenges and to deliver on them.

Team Objectives

A team needs an objective, a reason for existence. Without an objective how can the team members know they have completed their job? How can managers be sure the team are doing valuable work rather than just wasting time? The objective set for a team helps to give the team focus and helps the team leader to direct energies to particular tasks. As the team is likely to be in place for an extended period of time, the objective helps ensure that progress is made towards an overall goal. Without an objective, people can wander from the subject and lose sight of why the team was formed in the first place.

The objectives being set for the team need to be:

- **Realistic:** There is little point in asking a newly formed team to solve problems that are unrealistic. The scale and scope of the problem to be tackled needs to be matched with the resources devoted to it.

- **Achievable:** The team should have a reasonable chance of success. If management sets the goals too high, then the team is unlikely to achieve them. A failure at the early stages of team-building has negative long-term implications. It is generally better to set a slightly lower goal and to ,achieve it than to set a very high goal and fail.

- **Demanding:** While the goals being set for the team should not be set too high, they need to be set high enough to ensure that staff will have to work to achieve them. If the goal is too low, then people are unlikely to engage with the process.

Team Meetings

The team needs to meet, to discuss progress, develop action plans, to talk through problems encountered and successes achieved. The meetings should be kept relatively short and structured. The use of a simple agenda, recording action points, progress and future activities can be helpful.

Meetings can serve three very useful purposes:

- Report on action to date.
- Discuss potential solutions to outstanding problems.
- Plan future action.

The leader should focus the meetings on identifying solutions, as a team, to outstanding issues. The meetings can also be used to develop a team understanding of key tools and techniques as they become relevant.

The meetings should be kept relatively informal at the early stages of the process, in an effort to build a group approach to problem-solving. As the team develops, and people learn how to work together, the process can move to being more formal, with minutes and detailed agenda items. Minutes should be short, to the point and focused on directing future activity, and should be issued very soon after the meeting, not later than next day if at all possible.

Team Assignments

Teams are created to *do* things, to deliver on specific objectives and to achieve goals. A team of people that meet, discuss problems and do not deliver on them is just another waste in a business. Once the objectives of the team have been set, it should become possible to identify specific tasks and actions that need to be completed before the objectives can be achieved.

Specific tasks need to be assigned to individual team members or pairs of members. These people then have the responsibility to deliver on these tasks to, and for, the team. By harnessing the energies of several people to different facets of the problem, the team can deliver results more quickly than any one individual could.

The order in which tasks are tackled, and the priorities given to the tasks, needs to be discussed and agreed at the team meetings. This approach ensures that a coherent response is developed, and that everybody knows how their individual efforts will contribute to achieving the overall objectives of the team.

Team Results and Reviews

The results and progress being made by the team need to be reviewed regularly. This review should take place at two levels:

- Within the team itself.
- By senior management.

The team needs to be aware of the results it is achieving. The team should not have to wait for management, or the finance department,, or any other outside element of the organisation to tell them whether they are performing well or achieving positive results. This self-review should be incorporated into the regular team meetings and become a natural part of the team's activities. As the team reaches the objectives and goals set for it, they have the opportunity of suggesting even higher objectives based on their shared learning and the benefit of the experience they have gained as a team.

The second level of results review should take place between the team and senior management. If management felt it important enough to commit company staff and resources to tackle a problem by forming a team, then management should be interested in the progress of the team. Management should seek to review progress, to be informed of actions taken and results achieved. Management should be interested enough in the activities of the team to ask about future activities and when and how the team sees itself achieving its objectives. Management need to care about the progress of the team and need to let the team members know that they care. Some managers fall into the trap of derogating responsibility for the team and its objectives completely to the team leader. While this is legitimate up to a point, managers still need to demonstrate that the efforts of the team are aligned with the overall objectives of the business and that the team's efforts are both worthwhile and valued.

The team, along with management, should identify a number of key measures that can be used to monitor progress. These measures need to be chosen carefully to ensure that they are a true indicator of progress and also that, by achieving improvement in them, no other adverse affects are felt by the business.

There are a number of general points to be made about data and measures:

- **Record Data** – The systematic capture of data from processes can help focus attention of staff on the facts of a business. By recording say, "sales per day", people can be directed towards identifying ways of achieving improvement. The old adage "What get measured improves" is still true.

- **Analyse Data** – Look for information from the raw data. Are there patterns? What do the numbers show? By choosing carefully what data is recorded, new ways to improve the operation can be found. The needs and desires of customers can often provide a guide to what should be measured. Are clients focused on timeliness of delivery, superior quality or purely on price?

- **Use Data** – If people have gone to the bother of identifying good measures for the team's work, it is vitally important to act based on the results and data captured. The data is useful to the business only when used to further improve the operations.

BRAINSTORMING

Brainstorming is one of the most widely known tools used by teams. The approach is based on the positive interaction between team members when focused on tackling particular problems or issues. The team is brought together usually in a relatively confined space and is given a limited amount of time to focus on particular aspects of the problem.

A number of conditions need to be set before a team can embark on a successful brainstorming session:

1. All team members are equal. Normal levels of status within the organisation should be suspended during the session. Each member of the team has a potentially equal contribution to make.

2. All ideas are equal. The process, at least in the first phase, is non-judgemental. Ideas are sought without determining whether they are practical or even feasible. Experience has shown that an idea that was, of itself, impractical can often lead to the creation of another feasible idea that might not otherwise have arisen.

3. All comments must be positive. The process is designed to help the team identify and capture ideas. There is an onus on all team members to be positive towards each other and their suggestions. The time for critical analysis is during phase two of the process.

Armed with these general conditions, the team can move to initiate their brainstorming activity. It is generally necessary to remove the team from distractions during the process. This is often best achieved by bringing the teams "off-site", away from the daily demands of business. At a minimum, the session should take place in a room without telephones and without a window overlooking the operation.

The full brainstorming process consists of three distinct phases: Idea Generation; Critical Analysis; and Implementation Planning.

Phase I – Idea Generation

The idea generation phase is the core of creativity in the brainstorming process. The objective is to focus the creative energy of the team on finding ideas that may contribute to solving the problems facing the team. The problem(s) to be addressed are written on flipchart sheets, usually attached to the walls of the room so that they are in view to the team members. Even though they may not be concentrating on the sheets, the sheets often act as triggers for further ideas.

The brainstorming session should be time limited, typically to 20 to 30 minutes per creative session. The leader of the session usually has a number of ideas to start the process and they work with the other team members to draw out ideas and suggestions from all the team members. The task of writing suggestions on the flipcharts should be shared between a number of people, to both facilitate participation and also to give the writer a break.

It is typical that refreshments be brought to the brainstorming room rather than breaking for food. This forced proximity with the team and the problem helps engender a highly focused environment, conducive to the generation of ideas.

When the flow of ideas has dried up, and the leader feels that a reasonable number of ideas or suggestions have been gathered, the first phase can be drawn to a conclusion.

Phase II – Critical Analysis

The brainstorming team has now created a number of sheets containing ideas and suggestions. Some of these may be very practical, some may not. Phase II focuses on rating the ideas.

A simple rating system looks at the ideas under four headings:

1. **Definites:** Ideas that can, and should, be implemented immediately. These ideas are immediately beneficial and often arise simply by giving people the opportunity to make suggestions or through the interaction between people from different areas of the business.
2. **Probables:** Ideas that probably would work and be of benefit, but which require some further study or development before they could be implemented.
3. **Possibles:** These ideas may or may not work. They may have some chance of success but it is unlikely.
4. **Unlikelys:** Generally, off-the-wall ideas that have arisen during the session. While being unlikely in themselves, they may have contributed to the thought process of the team and helped to release other more likely suggestions.

When the team has rated the ideas, they move on to Phase III.

Phase III – Implementation Planning

"An idea that is not acted upon is a lost opportunity." The team has rated the ideas and will generally focus on those rated a "Definite" or a "Probable". The challenge now facing the team is to prioritise the ideas, and to identify the necessary time and resources required to move from the ideas stage to implementation.

The team will develop an implementation plan that will identify resources and responsibilities. The plan grows to become the action plan for the team and can provide both the team and management with a clear and measurable plan for action.

Getting Close to the Action

While brainstorming usually takes place in a closed environment, away from the distractions of the day job, another approach can also work. Bring the team to the problem. Bringing the team to the office area, the sales area, the manufacturing area or wherever area the problem exists can often help people to understand the issues clearly. Some people, particularly general office staff or shop floor workers, find it more effective and efficient to demonstrate the practical issues they face in the delivery of their job than to try and vocalise the issues.

Practical experience has shown that bringing the team to the problem can be very effective. People can see clearly that the daily problems they are experiencing and dealing with are receiving attention and they can often contribute further ideas to solve the problem.

14: WORLD CLASS SALES

How do you sell? Do you have a technique? Are you a "happy chappie" who talks about the match and takes an order or are you the serious type who focuses only on the technical aspects of your service or product and the customer's needs? If there is more than one person selling for an organisation, is there a common understanding of what the business sells and how to sell it?

It is often thought that selling is a black art. Yes, there are some really exceptional sales people but there are also many ordinary people who can benefit from the application of some "science" to the "art" of selling.

Put simply, a Company sells its services or products to a Customer, against Competitors and in a specific environment, or Community, as shown in **Figure 61**.

FIGURE 61: SALES STRATEGY

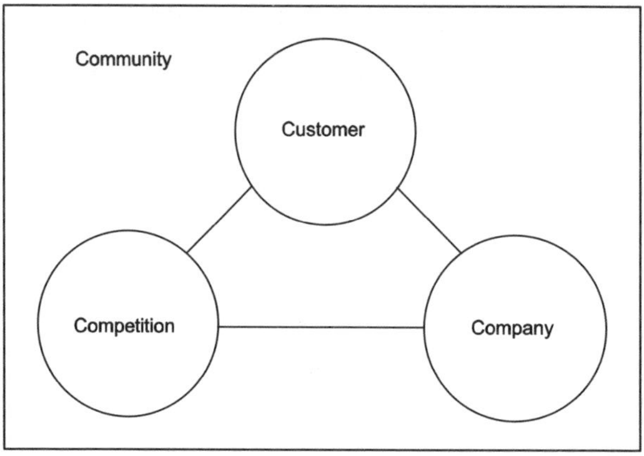

We will now look at each of these four "Cs" to understand better how World Class principles can be applied to the sales process.

YOUR COMPANY

One of the most basic elements of any good sales process is that the sales person needs to know and understand the product, the offering and the capabilities of the business. Unless the sales person knows these details, they are likely to over- or under-sell the business and the offering.

This knowledge requirement can be addressed through the use of a company profile sheet, as in **Figure 62**.

FIGURE 62: COMPANY PROFILE

Location:
No. of Employees:
Turnover:
Profit:

Good Points
Key Products Product Mfg. Process Sales/Mkt. Finance
1.
2.
3.

Weak Points
Key Products Product Mfg. Process Sales/Mkt. Finance
1.
2.
3.

Key Actions
1.
2.
3.

The company profile sheet captures key facts about the business. By looking at the key products or services and seeking to find strengths and weaknesses in them, an objective picture of the offering is formed. The focus on particular aspects of the product or service – such as the product itself, a uniqueness in manufacturing, special market position or financial advantage such as cost – helps the individuals in the business to look again at what they already "know" about the product or service. If a number of people complete the profile sheet independently of each other and then review the sheets together, different opinions are likely to be expressed regarding strengths and weaknesses. These differences of opinion can provide a very rich opportunity for discussion and can often lead to the identification of key actions.

The profile sheet ends with a list of key actions. The whole world class approach is focused on improvement – this is equally relevant in the sales process. The identification of key actions can be the accentuation of positive points or the minimisation of weaknesses. Quite often, the actions are a combination of both.

The detail of the headings under strengths and weaknesses will depend on what type of business is being run. Obviously, a service company will not have manufacturing as a heading and may substitute customer service for this heading. The decision as to what headings should be included in the profile sheet can form the basis for a worthwhile discussion, helping people to focus objectively on the business as an entity, an entity that can be improved. Additional information can be appended to the profile sheet as more detail on the business is gathered – outlining, for example, process capabilities, assets, and competitive advantages.

Before we move on to look at customer, competitor and community profiles, let's look at both Product Lists and Customer Lists, to capture an overview of the current situation for the business.

PRODUCT LIST

Few businesses have a single product. In general, business sales are made up by a range of products or services or at least from a set of variations on the basic offering. The product list captures information on these offerings with a view to identifying which products are of most significance to the business, as in **Figure 63**.

FIGURE 63: PRODUCT LIST

Product	Sales Value Last Year	Profit	Difficulty	Rating
1.				
2.				
3.				
4.				
5.				
6.				
7.				

The product list should include all major products as well as identifying variations. In some businesses, the Product List can run to several pages. All the variety of offerings should be listed to show the levels of complexity inherent in such cases.

The Product List seeks to capture sales value, as well as profitability per model or at least contribution levels. The "Difficulty" column seeks to determine just how difficult it is for the business to offer that particular service or product. The "Rating" column is once again relatively subjective. The aim is to balance profitability, volume and difficulty to identify priorities for focus for the business.

CUSTOMER LIST

The Customer List format is very similar to the Product List. The list seeks to identify a rating for customers to allow a degree of classification to be applied, as in **Figure 64**.

Sales volume and profitability measures can help in this classification process. By applying the Pareto principle, customers can be classified as A, B, or C type. The objective once again is to help a business prioritise its limited resources, to identify classes of customers or areas of business that are both high volume and high profitability, and to help identify areas for future potential growth based on the shared experience of the members of the business.

FIGURE 64: CUSTOMER LIST

Customer	Sales Value Last Year	Profit	Difficulty of Doing Business	Rating
1.				
2.				
3.				
4.				
5.				
6.				
7.				

A Customer List can usually be generated from the accounts system by listing customers in terms of annual sales invoiced. This data can then be added to, in order to address the other areas listed on the Customer List.

Customer Profile

It really is important to know who the customers are. Many people sell to the *wants* of their customers but seldom address their *needs*. If only customers' wants are addressed, then there is a risk of missing their needs and leaving the door open to the competition. Customer needs can be determined only through discussion with, and analysis of, customers. In the long-term, selling to meet customer needs is the only sustainable approach.

The Customer Profile sheet is a useful tool in helping determine the needs of clients. Many sales people feel they "know" their clients and have no need to commit this knowledge to paper. However, many of the best sales people keep this information in personal files. If the business is to grow and develop, a shared understanding of the customer base needs to be developed. The Customer Profile sheet helps with this process, as in **Figure 65**.

The sheet seeks to capture some basic information on key customers, such as where they are located, how many people they employ as well, as estimates of annual turnover and profitability. Information on what products or services they bought last year is also useful, along with an estimate of their expected purchasing in the year ahead. The objective is to arrive at a "Rating" for the customer. This rating is an indication of how important, or otherwise, the customer is to the business. The overall objective is clearly to provide the business with an objective, consensus view on a priority list of customers.

FIGURE 65: CUSTOMER PROFILE

Customer Name: **Rating:**

Location:

No. of Employees

Tel:

Fax:

E-mail:

Web:

Turnover (estimated):

Profit: (estimated):

Key Products/Services Last Year This Year Potential

1.

2.

3.

4.

5.

6.

7.

Customer profile sheets should be completed at least for the business' top customers, the top 20% of customers who account for 80% of sales, the "A" customers. These can easily be identified by referring to the "Customer List."

If there are other customers who could grow to significance, then it is obviously worthwhile to include them in the process and prepare customer profiles for them also.

COMPETITOR PROFILE

The Competitor Profile is largely based on the same format as the Company Profile. The sheet captures the same data but this time for key competitors. The objectivity of the process can often help identify weaknesses in a competitor's service or product offering that were not previously obvious. In some cases, the sharing of information on competitors in this structured way can lead to the piecing together of different elements of a jigsaw. When everybody's little piece of the puzzle is brought together, a clear picture of the true level of competition can be gained.

The objectives of the process are:

1. To understand the competition in comparison to the company itself.
2. To pool the knowledge held within different elements of the business.
3. To plan responses to tackle the competition in an effective and efficient way.

The competition is just that, competition for business. They are trying to take sales away from our business – the winner is the one who takes most!

COMMUNITY PROFILE

The Community Profile, or environmental analysis, is possibly the hardest profile sheet to complete. We seldom try to foretell the future and this is what we are trying to do. By limiting the view forward to three to five years, we have a better chance of getting predictions right. For example, changes in European Community laws do not arrive overnight – there is usually a significant period of discussion and consultation as changes are proposed. It is important to be aware of changes as they are being proposed if they could affect, either positively or negatively, one's future business potential.

The increasing emphasis on environmental control and pollution minimisation is a case in point. For many businesses, these changes in the law simply add to the burden of doing business while, for a small number of other businesses, they provide a source of new sales opportunities.

By looking at social and economic factors, it may be possible to identify in advance potential changes in market demand. The demographics in Ireland indicate that the 50+ year-old market will become very significant over the coming years with related business potential. Such changes in demographics and buying power can lead to real market opportunities. The challenge is to identify these opportunities and prepare an offering to benefit from them.

Case Study: Richard Keenan & Co Ltd

Richard Keenan & Co Ltd was established in 1979. It is a family-owned business employing 200 people. Keenan's exports to markets in Europe, Australia, South Africa, Argentina and the US. Expansion into new markets was partly a response to the BSE crisis, which hit sales in Europe, especially in the UK.

The company is rightly proud of what it calls "the Keenan way" of doing business. A key differentiator is the high emphasis on customer care. If a feeder unit breaks down (which is rare as the units are very reliable), the Keenan charter guarantees that full service will be restored in one day anywhere in the world.

The core product is a highly-reliable total mixed ration (TMR) feeder unit. In addition, Keenan's has 25 full-time nutritionists who ensure the customer understands how to optimise feeder unit performance.

The Probe benchmarking exercise and diagnostic analysis identified a number of issues preventing the company from achieving its objectives. A cross functional team was established to identify the obstacles, and to propose/implement actions to achieve a 10% increase in sales in 1998.

Data was captured, showing that some sales representatives had a 50% hit rate – they received one order per two site visits. The average hit rate was 20%. One action was to identify and document the successful formula used by the high hit rate sales people. A new sales manual was prepared and a major training exercise was undertaken for all sales staff. Improvements were made to the customer database, and improved prospect tracking systems put in place. A new system to improve the quality of product and site specifications was introduced. As a result, sales increased by 25% in the first year. Since 1998, sales have grown from 700 units per year to 1,300 units per year.

The company initiated projects in other areas of the business to support the increased sales – particularly in purchasing and just-in-time manufacture. Gains were achieved, leading to reduced shortages on the line, giving increased productivity to meet the extra sales. Significant savings have been made in purchasing. Projects on value analysis and automatic welding were also initiated and major cost reductions are expected to accrue from these. The company has a top class management team, which now has a new confidence in its ability to build a more sustainable competitive advantage by continuous improvement using the principles of world class business.

PROFILE ANALYSIS

The work of preparing profiles on the company, Customers, Competitors and Community has been done. The time for analysis is now. The use of visual techniques can help here.

Attach the Company Profile to a wall. On one side of it, attach the key Customer Profiles. On the other side, attach the Competitor Profiles. Below, attach the Community Profile. The opportunity now exists to study the information gathered, as in **Figure 66**.

FIGURE 66: PROFILE ANALYSIS

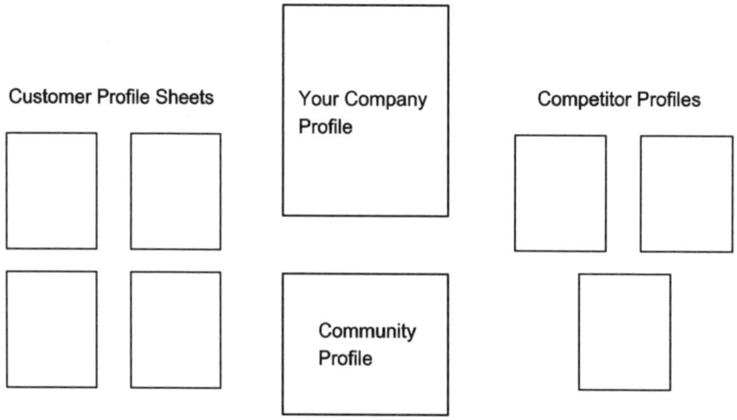

The primary objective of the exercise is to increase sales and profitability. A commonly-accepted fact of sales is that it is very much harder to get a new customer than it is to sell to an existing one. An analysis of the Customer Profiles may lead to the realisation that some existing customers are not buying all of the range of products that they could. The opportunity may arise either to increase the range of product being sold to individual customers or to offer higher margin products.

Turning attention to the Competitor profiles, it should be possible to identify action items, where advantage can be taken in the market. By examining the key customers serviced by the competition, it may be possible to identify prospects, customers who already have a need for a product similar to those that the business can supply but who are buying from others. Care needs to be exercised as to how competitors are tackled; if they are stronger, then care needs to be taken to avoid "enraging the bull" rather than securing new business.

The last part of the puzzle relates to the Community Profile. By looking at this profile, it may be possible to identify strategic decisions and directions that the company need to take.

COMPETITIVE ANALYSIS

The Company and Competitor Analysis sheets can be used to start the process of competitive analysis. To take customers from competitors, it is essential that competitive advantage is identified in your offerings. The Competitive Analysis sheet helps with this process (see **Figure 67**).

The competitive analysis process is widely used by major corporations. A joke in the automotive industry is that the first 10 cars from any production run are not bought by customers but by competitors. These cars are then tested and dis-assembled to see what new ideas have been developed. The objective is not simply to copy but to learn from others – by examining carefully the solutions of others to innovate further and build increased functionality or performance into products.

A good starting point for competitive analysis is the advertising materials, brochures and specification sheets produced by competitors. Careful study of these can often challenge a team to deliver at least as good performance as the competition.

FIGURE 67: COMPETITIVE ANALYSIS

	Est. Sales	Est. Mkt. Position	Key Features
Competitor 1.			
Competitor 2.			
Competitor 3.			
Your Company			

Areas of Competitive Advantage
A.
B.
C.

Areas of Competitive Disadvantage
A.
B.
C.

Actions Identified	**Priority**
1.	
2.	
3.	

The Competitive Analysis process should not be limited to sales and marketing staff but should be a team-based activity involving sales, design, purchasing, production and finance staff. This team approach will help ensure that a company-wide response to the challenge of competitors is realised. Take the opportunity to scrutinise competitor products at trade fairs and exhibitions and try to identify both strengths and weaknesses of their product, their service or their companies. The challenge is to attack weaknesses and find defences against their strengths.

The "market worth" tool can be useful when trying to understand market conditions and the relative positions of competitors and competing products. An example of how this tool is used is presented in both tabular and graphical forms in **Figure 68**.

FIGURE 68: MARKET WORTH

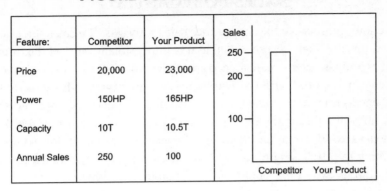

Feature:	Competitor	Your Product
Price	20,000	23,000
Power	150HP	165HP
Capacity	10T	10.5T
Annual Sales	250	100

This analysis indicates that the market prefers cheap price to higher specifications, or at least is not prepared to pay much of a premium for those additional features.

SALES MANUAL

The sales process can be developed and improved. The creation of a sales manual can often help salespeople to reach an acceptable level of performance within a reasonable time. Much of the material already gathered is used as a basis for the manual.

At a minimum, the manual should contain:

- Company Profile
- Customer Needs, issues and possible solutions
- Competitor profiles, identifying strengths and weaknesses
- Technical data and Comparison sheets
- Specification sheets, identifying key order parameters to ensure that the product ordered and delivered are correct.
- Options lists
- Pricing information and conditions of trade.

SALES FORECASTING

Very few salespeople like to produce sales forecasts. If a sales forecast is asked for, the likely response is that it is impossible to predict the future, so it is impossible to create an accurate sales forecast. However, how can purchasing or production or warehousing staff have products ready for sale unless they have some forward visibility of market requirements? If it is not possible for the sales people to produce a forecast, given their closeness to the market, then it is even less possible for someone working in purchasing to do so. The logical conclusion to this argument is to quote extra-long lead-times to customers, allowing orders to be placed for parts only when customers place an order or to hold large stocks of parts. Neither solution is favoured by the majority of businesses. It is a necessary fact of life that sales forecasts are made.

In an effort to start the forecasting process, past sales history can be helpful. The previously created Products List can provide this. The question should be asked whether history is likely to repeat itself, or have factors changed that will significantly change likely sales into the future. Has a new competitor joined the market or have innovative new products been introduced? Will sales promotions be repeated or will new ones be introduced? These factors should be used to modify, if necessary, the sales history information.

The question of what sales are forecast for the coming year can also be asked from this starting point. The creation of an annual sales forecast is useful for purchasing, manufacturing and logistics personnel. It helps them plan for the future with suppliers as well as preparing staff and equipment. However, the annual sales forecast is of little benefit as a regular management tool. Sales management needs to be more immediate and in better control than that allowed by an annual sales forecast.

The forecasting and management of the sales process should happen on a regular basis – daily, weekly or monthly, depending on the type of business. Some businesses, in particular the fast moving consumer goods industry, even measure sales per hour rates. In a more typical environment, weekly monitoring of sales made and prospects forward is usually sufficient. Prospects should be rated, say as ABC, with A prospects being likely to convert to sales and C prospects those who are less likely as short-term sales. Reviews should take place quickly and regularly of progress towards targets and movement on the prospects list. Bar charts can be used quite effectively to monitor progress towards overall targets with weekly sales or individual sales being recorded, depending on the culture of the business (see **Figure 69**).

FIGURE 69: SALES TARGETS

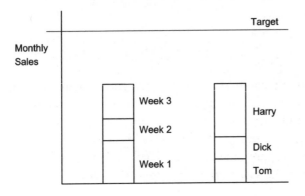

It is essential to review forecast *versus* actual accuracy levels regularly. There is no point in individual sales people forecasting huge sales levels and not delivering on them. By the same token, the opposite situation is almost as bad, where sales are forecast low. In either situation, procurement, production and logistics staff will encounter severe problems of too much or too little stock or time to produce. Here again, the use of a run chart can be very helpful, to record the level of accuracy of forecast *versus* actual sales. Since it is unrealistic in many businesses to expect forecast accuracies of better than five to 10 percent, it is useful to set target lines for accuracy on the chart, as in **Figure 70**.

FIGURE 70: FORECAST ACCURACY

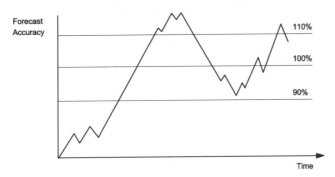

Charting customer sales patterns was discussed earlier. It can often be very helpful to customers, as well as the business, if customers can be provided with a pattern of their consumption as well as suggesting ways to reduce costs along the supply chain between the supplier and the customer.

ACTIVITY PLANNING

When planning a sales strategy, including sales activities, it is important to create an overall plan using a diary. Are there specific events taking place, key industry sector shows or other such activities that require a presence? It is important to spread activities over the year rather than having them all grouped into one particular part of the year, unless, of course, the business is purely time dependent and limited.

The primary goal of such activities is to bring the company and its offering into the minds of customers and prospective customers, and to keep it there. For example, one of the world's largest advertisers is Coca Cola, which constantly reinforces the brand with existing and new customers.

The sales activities should be balanced, including, say, golf or match outings, trade shows and exhibitions, articles in trade journals, advertising and even sponsorship. It is important to capture feedback from customers as to the effectiveness of the activity invested in. There is little point in inviting a customer to a soccer match if they hate the sport. By capturing customer feedback, an activity plan can be developed for future years, working to achieve a positive return from the investment of time and effort.

TARGETING CUSTOMERS

It is usually easier to gain more business from existing customers than it is to capture new ones. Therefore, it is often worth examining what level and type of business is being done with existing customers and work to maximise this business first. It is helpful to understand the abilities of the business and target sectors or customers where the business has a proven expertise.

When new customers need to be targeted, it is often worthwhile to return to the Competitor Profile sheets. Are there customers one is doing business with that could be targeted? Set a goal of identifying and securing a specific number of new customers per operating period.

When new prospects have been identified, it is useful to prepare a Customer Profile sheet for them. Identify, as best as possible, what is important to each customer, what they are looking for that the competition is not providing. Then the business must be challenged to see if it can service this need. There is no point in making service or product promises that the company will not be able to meet. There is no point, and indeed a lot of negativity, in raising customer expectations unless they can be met.

Having identified prospects, their needs and the ability to service them, it is time to develop a plan of attack. It is important to be prepared for the response of prospective customers who may look for samples. By preparing for these eventualities, the business will be able to project a professional and efficient image of the business.

MEASURES FOR THE SALES TEAM

The use of measures can be helpful when it comes to managing a sales team. Is the salesperson who spends all their time in the car being effective? Is there an opportunity to learn from the best members of the sales team, by sharing and developing a company-wide sales process?

Some of the more obvious measures are those that relate to personal sales made, which are easily tracked, using a run chart to check patterns over time and also in bar chart form to see progress towards a target level. The overall sales level can also be tracked in this way.

An additional twist to sales measurement looks at the variation between list price and actual sales price invoiced. If there is a significant differential, maybe the list price is too high or maybe margin is being given away too easily. At least, by measuring the differential, attention will be drawn to the issue.

Back to our friend in the car. A simple but very interesting measure for someone managing a sales team is the measure of sales made per mile driven. This is an effectiveness measure and can often be useful in helping sales staff realise opportunities for a more focused approach to selling.

Finally, forecast accuracy is a very important measure from the point of view of the overall business. Sales forecasts should be driven towards being more accurate and also driven to meet the growth needs of the business, putting pressure on sales, design, manufacturing, procurement and logistics staff to meet them.

CUSTOMER SERVICE

Customers have now been landed, so it is essential that the business meet their expectations by providing them with a quality service.

Each customer is different. It is important to recognise these differences and ensure that systems are developed enough to ensure that each customer needs are met. Key measures should be identified, used and tracked to record performance and developments made in the area of customer service. Such measures as On Time Deliveries, Customer Complaints, Completed *vs.* Partial Orders and Paperwork complaints could be tracked and publicised as part of the improvement activities.

As improvements are made in each key area, communicate these to customers and enter into a dialogue to determine how the process can be improved further. This dialogue with customers builds relationships that raise the entry barriers to other competitors. The challenge is to improve the level of operational capability to the point where the business is truly world class, offering services and products to its customers Quicker, Better and Cheaper. If that is the case, then the customers will stay with the business.

15: FINANCIAL MANAGEMENT

Money is important, and the effective and efficient management of money is essential in a competitive business. It is essential that companies using World Class Business techniques use and develop their understanding of financial matters to ensure the development of their businesses. Too often, financial accounts are left unused. Too often, the insights that even a simple analysis of these figures could give are left unseen. This section cannot cover the full extent of financial analysis or financial management but it aims to de-mystify some of the terms used and show how additional value can be gained from professionally-prepared accounts.

As with many aspects of WCB, the objective when using financial analysis is to gain a better understanding of the business, how it is progressing and to try to see danger signs at the earliest possible time. If developing danger can be seen, then counter-measures can be taken, the earlier the better.

This section looks at some of the financial ratios often used by financial analysts, bankers and investors. The effects of a WCB initiative on the measures a company can use to monitor performance are also addressed.

RATIO ANALYSIS

If the business has ever applied for a loan or sought to interest an investor in taking a stake, then it has most likely been subjected to Ratio Analysis. Since the end of the 1800s, when large amounts of capital were required to develop America, Ratio Analysis has been used to determine whether a particular investment proposal was worthwhile. A series of ratios have grown out of this activity.

One key point to remember is that no single measure is enough to determine the performance of a business. A good analyst will identify a number of relevant measures, for a given sector or business type, and will also be very interested in trends over time. In order to get meaningful results, at least three years' accounting information is required – two sets of audited accounts provides this.

Key Operational Ratios

Turnover per Employee = Sales Revenue / no. employees

Profit per Employee = (Profit before Interest and Tax) / no. employees

Value added per Employee = (Sales Revenue – Cost of materials) / no. employees

These three ratios seek to understand how efficient the business is with its people, and how effective. The first of these measures is often the easiest one to calculate. It gives an indication to the level of effectiveness of staff, and the systems they operate. The absolute figure is not really that important, the norms vary from sector to sector. Management should be focussed on achieving improvements in this ratio, over time. Leading companies, worldwide, achieve improvements in this ratio of 15% to 20%, per annum.

The second ratio, that of Profit per employee, is a challenging measure, especially for companies looking to employ additional staff, particularly in management, support or indirect functions. The challenge is to ensure that the addition of extra payroll costs leads to an improvement in overall profitability.

The third ratio, value added per employee, is a hard measure, especially for sales-oriented businesses or those with a mixture of sales and manufacturing. Stripping out the cost of materials helps focus business attention on what is important for long-term sustainability. If the value-add is low, the challenge is to increase it. This can often lead to the identification of a need to develop new or innovative products or services. If the value-add is high, then the challenge can often be how to protect the business from competitors who may want to take such valuable business away.

Stock Turnover

Stock turnover is easy to calculate and is a good measure of the efficiency of a business to process materials. The higher the level of stock turns, the more efficient the business is in turning materials into value-added finished goods. The best manufacturing companies in the world turn stock 50 to 100 times per year.

Opening Stock = A
Closing Stock = B
Subtotal = A + B
Average Stock = (A+B)/2
Stock turnover = Cost of Sales / Average Stock

A focus on stock turns can help in the development of stores/materials-logistics staff. Also, it can help identify the need to develop suppliers. If suppliers can deliver based on real needs, then there will be little need to keep large stocks. The measure can also help challenge assumptions in terms of sales and help as a focus in the development of worthwhile and accurate forecasts. It should be obvious that, if forecasts are wildly inaccurate, then it will be very difficult for stores staff or suppliers to meet market sales demands without keeping large stocks. Remember, time is money and the longer stock is held, the lower the stock turns number will be and the more costly it will be to run and develop the business.

Debtor Days

This measure looks at how good the business is at getting paid for its efforts. It determines the number of days before getting paid. The larger the number, the slower customers are to pay. The debtor days ratio is calculated as follows:

$$Debtor\ Days = Debtors/(Sales/365)$$

It represents the average collection period. In simple terms, if the debtor days ratio is high, the business is financing its customers' businesses, by providing its own money to help them to do business. Even worse, it could be borrowing money from a bank to finance its customers' businesses.

The use of Pareto Analysis is recommended on debtors. Are all customers are slow to pay, or is there a clearly identifiable core of slow payers? If such a "slow core" can be identified, then the challenge facing the business is to find a way to either redress this situation or to find replacement customers. The alternative – a costly one – is to continue to provide a quasi-banking service to its customers. If the problem is because of poor systems in the accounts area, then this is an issue to be tackled. The introduction of Debtor Days as a management metric can often result, in and of itself, an improvement in performance in this centrally important area.

Creditor Days

The balance to debtor days is Creditor Days. This is a measure of the time it takes you to pay your suppliers and is calculated as follows:

$$\text{Creditor Days} = \text{Creditors}/(\text{Purchases}/365)$$

If the creditor days figure is lower than debtor days, then the business is financing its customers' businesses. A fine balancing act needs to take place between these two ratios. The closer the ratios are and the lower the absolute number for each, the better the situation.

By paying creditors on time one can usually expect, and demand, a good service level. If a business gets the reputation as a poor payer, then it becomes very difficult to expect good service or help and support with supplier development activities.

Supermarkets' customers, pay on receipt of goods while their creditors deliver at short notice and on 30+ day terms of payment. A well-run supermarket can make significant contribution to profit, based on this margin between money coming in and money going out.

The challenge for businesses generally is to close this gap between debtors and creditors days ratios, to recognise cash as an asset, and to manage this asset effectively.

Other Key Operational Ratios

A number of other financial ratios can be very useful to the non-financial manager:

- Sales or Turnover Growth
- Wages or Direct Labour Growth
- Materials Purchase Growth
- Overhead Growth
- Debtors to Revenue Growth
- Creditors to Revenue Growth
- Net Assets Growth.

The Key Factor with all these ratios is the growth or change in the measure over time. If wages are growing faster than turnover, there may be a problem. Similarly for the other metrics. These metrics are relatively easy to capture and to track over time. Their use can be very helpful in the early identification of problems within a business.

Case Study: PB Machine Tech Ltd

PB Machine Tech. Ltd. is an engineering company involved in the production of made-to-order, standard products and special purpose machines for domestic timber processing. The company has focused heavily on dedicated machine centres and has a high level of expertise and capability in the areas of sub-contract machining. The company had no firm costing and quoting system in place, was suffering from low production efficiency and had no means of recording downtime.

Actions Taken

The company developed a reporting system that captured production levels achieved and downtimes incurred. It issued this sheet on a daily basis to staff and used it as the basis for payment calculations. Management wanted to be able to see whether individual products made a profit or a loss. They wanted to:

- Feed the quoting system from the costing system.
- Minimise the downtime in production, ideally at little investment.
- Know where costs were being incurred, in labour or materials.

The objective was to identify jobs where materials contents were costed correctly, where the labour content was accurately estimated but the sales price for the product was not producing a profit. This analysis would lead to the identification of products that should be dropped or where the customer should be asked for a price increase. In addition, this process was also seen to provide the opportunity to identify products where the margins could be improved by re-examining the machining process and other operations.

The sheets also recorded machine downtimes. These results were then used to feed the production manager to help improve process.

Although it takes about one hour a day to input all the sheets, the new system is providing real data and significant improvement.

Results Achieved

- Initially, the company hoped to be able to cost three to four jobs per week. It can now cost every job, with the costing available on the Tuesday of the following week for the previous week's production.
- Output per man is up by 20%.
- A scheduling system for prioritising jobs at saws has lead to improved service levels for the three departments drawing materials from the saw area.
- Trolley for sawn parts, where the saw man cuts parts and fills the trolley, before it is transported to the machine shop, welder etc. saves lots of time.
- Tools are racked and labelled for ease of access and traceability, with tool storage at machines.
- A mobile consumable store put in place, so machine operators now do not have to go to Stores and consumables use has been reduced also.
- Charts are displayed on wall to indicate actual performance of the company.
- Improved management capability.
- Importance of team activities realised by management.

Financiers' Ratios

The ratios discussed so far are of an operational nature – they can help a manager to run his or her business in an effective way. There are a number of measures that are often used by financial institutions or investors if they are examining a business. It is worthwhile for a manager to be aware of these measures to understand how a bank or external agency, or potential investor, will examine the business based on its financial data.

Return on Net Assets (RONA)

RONA examines how effective a business is at generating wealth, a return on the investment made. It is calculated as follows:

$$RONA = \frac{\text{Profit Before Interest \& Taxes}}{\text{Net Assets}}$$

The key to the use of RONA as a measure is to examine the cost of debt *versus* the RONA metric being recorded. If a company borrows capital at, say, 10% and its RONA figure is 15%, then there is a positive margin of 5%. If the business has a RONA figure of less than 10%, its cost of capital, then it is effectively borrowing capital to lose it. In many businesses, RONA can be below the cost of capital in the general market. In such cases, if it were possible, the business would be better served to liquidate and invest the money in the capital markets.

Interest Cover

One of the first checks done by a prospective lender is on the level of Interest Cover. This is a simple calculation that examines the ability of the business to cover its debt payments and is calculated as:

$$\frac{\text{(Interest Costs \& Earnings before extraordinary items)} \times 100}{\text{Interest Costs}}$$

At its most basic level, the ratio should be over 100. If the ratio is less than 100, the business will be unable to meet its debt payments; at 100, it is just able to meet them. In normal circumstances, an analyst will look for a ratio of 300 to 400 when analysing a prospective client's accounts.

Liquidity Ratio

There are two liquidity ratios in general use:

- Current Ratio
- Acid Test Ratio.

The liquidity ratios examine a business' ability to meet its current liabilities. The ratios are calculated as follows:

Current Ratio = (Current Assets) / (Current Liabilities)

Acid Test Ratio = (Current Assets – Stock) / (Current Liabilities)

In general, the acid test ratio is more severe than the current ratio. Analysts typically look for a ratio of 1 or greater for this metric. The current ratio is usually targeted at 2 or greater. Specific sector and market norms are very important when using the liquidity ratios.

ACTIVITY BASED COSTING

Activity Based Costing seeks to help management understand the real costs associated with making a product or providing a service. Many costing systems allocate the general business overhead on an arbitrary basis – by number of employees, per square metre of floor space occupied or some other similarly arbitrary measure.

In a real life example, baby nappies were being made in a business unit, with two machines. One machine was over 10 years old, the other recently purchased. The old machine had a manning level higher than the theoretical manning level of the new machine. The old machine was very reliable and consistently produced 90,000 to 100,000 units per shift, every shift. The new machine produced 0 to 20,000 to 150,000 per shift, in no real pattern. The old machine was paid for and needed normal levels of maintenance. The new machine cost nearly €1 million and needed constant expensive maintenance. On an allocated cost basis, the new machine appeared cheaper than the old one – simply because it had lower manning levels. The reality was very different. Activity Based Costing seeks to allocate true costs to specific activities such as engineering, maintenance, support functions and consumed overhead.

The objective of Activity Based Costing is to provide management with real data on the actual costs being incurred on which to base decisions.

Activity Based Costing looks at costs at four different levels:
1. Unit Level Costs are those direct costs such as labour and materials and also machine-specific costs such as electricity and machine financing.
2. Batch Level Costs relate to costs directly attributable to producing a batch such as tool and jig purchasing, set-up time, inspection and testing costs, materials handling and scrap costs.
3. Product / Process Level Costs relate to items such as maintenance costs on machinery, changes to the product requiring engineering input, product development costs and yield losses inherent in the product.
4. Organisation Level Costs are business level costs related to staying in business such as depreciation, staff costs in administration, marketing and other functional departments.

The Activity Based Costing approach provides management with specific and focused insight into what is happening in an operation and where the money flows are. Decisions tend to be based on facts rather than opinion or very high-level information. Experience has shown that the application of WCB techniques, in conjunction with the Activity Based Costing approach, can often highlight the fact that products that seemed to be loss leaders can be developed into real stars.

Finally, remember that the cost to manufacture a product does not determine what the selling price should be. Selling price is most usually defined by competition, a market's ability or inclination to absorb a specific price level and by a business' aggression in that market. The use of Activity Based Costing and World Class Business and Benchmarking practices can help a business be more aggressive, as it moves to be more capable, rather than just having to give away margin in order to gain sales.

CONCLUSION

Financial analysis is a demanding and often quite sophisticated area of endeavour. The basic tools presented here can help a non-financial manager to understand some aspects of their business from the point of view of a financial person.

The use of selected key metrics can help bring objectivity to an operation and can provide an early warning to a management team of a change in circumstances. If managers are tuned to be aware of these changes, then they can take action to address them before serious issues develop.

These ratios need to be treated with caution and used carefully. No single measure can tell the full story of a business and they are most useful when used to map trends over time.

16: SUPPLY CHAIN & LOGISTICS

A company does not exist in a vacuum and few companies since Ford's Rouge plant make their products from iron ore upwards. Most companies are part of a supply chain, either relying on others to supply them with goods or supplying their products to others who rely on them. An analysis of the leading manufacturing companies in the world has shown that up to 85% of the cost of their products is bought in from other suppliers. So far, we have focused on building capability and effectiveness within a business. Now, let's look at the supply chain.

Realising that a business is part of a supply chain helps to understand the complexity of the business. We have already identified wastes in administration, product development, sales and manufacturing areas; now we will look for similar wastes in internal materials management and planning areas as well as with, and between, suppliers. The marketplace today demands short lead times and high levels of flexibility. A business can meet these demands either by holding large stock levels of finished goods and raw materials or by developing both internal capabilities and its relationships with its suppliers.

A business must identify those suppliers who:

- Can and do meet its requirements for superior service
- Could develop to meet these needs.
- Will not or cannot meet these needs.

Big and small businesses rely on supply chains for survival and growth. Like many other aspects of a World Class Business approach, until a focus is brought on to the facts relating to suppliers and the interactions with them, opinions will abound. Many companies continue to do business with poor quality suppliers over many years, because they often feel they have no choice. In many cases, they do have choices, just they do not seem to understand that they can take them.

Over the past 10 years, many larger companies have moved to develop their suppliers. They have taken the time to transfer technologies and understanding to them. In many cases, effectively, staff from the bigger companies have mentored the smaller companies. This transfer of knowledge and understanding was not done for any altruistic reason but for purely business ones. The bigger companies are moving up the value chain, seeking to add value to their products through high level design, system integration and customer service rather than through performing basic manufacturing operations.

Leading companies also have come to rely on smaller companies to provide expertise and innovation in particular aspects of their products. This transfer of responsibility to smaller companies has proven very beneficial for those companies that have risen to the challenge, and very difficult for those who have not. The arrangement along the supply chain is like a pyramid, as in **Figure 71**.

FIGURE 71: SUPPLY CHAIN

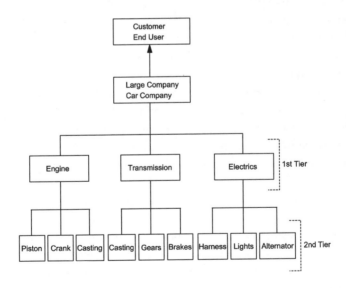

The car company deals with the customer or end-user and depends on its key, first-tier suppliers for major elements of its products. It also depends on them for levels of innovation in their particular areas of expertise. The first-tier company also relies on its suppliers for both product and innovation. For the pyramid to work, it is clear that all levels need to be working to the same standard, to be following the same road with similar objectives. It would be totally inappropriate to have a low-quality second-tier company working for a high-quality first-tier or end-user company.

The supply chain is simply a strand of the pyramid. We will now look at some of the key aspects of supply chain and how it relates to small and medium-sized companies.

PURCHASING – IS PRICE KING?

How many suppliers service the business? Are purchases made based on price, at a quality level of course? Or are such things as variety, service, flexibility, delivery and innovative ability taken into consideration?

By buying only on the basis of price, businesses often miss the opportunity to secure real competitive advantage. Currently, Eastern European and Far Eastern manufacturers are cheaper on price for a number of industrial commodities, at least when price alone is considered. Factor in lead-time, potential quality problems, high order quantities and possible transport difficulties and maybe the package as a whole is not so attractive. Would it be possible to develop a relationship with a local supplier, where the hidden costs of doing business between companies could be identified and removed, and which in turn would result in lower true pricing while retaining the competitive advantages that close proximity, flexibility and responsiveness can bring?

The Ford Motor Company prided itself on being a true world leader in terms of its purchasing practices. They believed that they "bought as well as the best", until they became involved with Mazda of Japan. When Ford looked at the number of people buying components per thousand cars produced, Mazda had only 20% of the staff Ford had employed in this role. The Japanese company was doing their purchasing in a different way, having developed a long-term relationship with the members of their pyramid, their suppliers.

The key here was "working together". Mazda and its suppliers had examined the purchasing process and the paper trail associated with it, from initial request for quotation to payment and credit note procedures, and had simplified the process. They removed wastes, thereby reducing costs.

One of the simplest examples of this was for the seat manufacturer. Rather than the seat manufacturer invoicing Mazda for individual consignments of seats for each car or batch of cars, Mazda paid the manufacturer based on the number of cars produced. Each car leaving the production line had to have seats, so the supplier was due to be paid for them. Thus, over time, both Mazda and their suppliers had developed trust and also basic systems of control to ensure fairness in their business transactions. Both benefited from the removal of unnecessary paperwork between their businesses. Needless to say Ford moved to learn more about the Mazda approach to procurement and worked to identify wastes along their own supply chain.

But price alone is not king. Some companies have created positions for themselves at the tops of pyramids, others populate the sides and foundation levels. Companies such as Ford, Toyota, Honda, and others depend on their suppliers to create innovations in the systems they fit to their cars. The supplier is given broad performance, cost and quality parameters and can then innovate within those boundaries. Small companies often tend to be very good at their specific business. They know a lot about the materials they use, the process they apply and how to maximise performance from their limited resources. Big companies rely on these abilities, and can often help small companies to understand and use systems to help them meet ever-increasing standards of quality. By working together, the full supply chain can benefit.

Case Study:
Erin Foods

Erin Foods manufactures a range of dried food products including soups, sauces and dried vegetables. It a very well-known and respected brand within Ireland. The company was formed as part of the semi-State sector and has been in operation for approximately 30 years. In the past five years, its ownership has transferred to the private sector, as part of the Greencore Group, formerly Irish Sugar. The workforce and management of the company came from a predominantly State sector orientation.

The company formed three multi-functional teams addressing the areas of Procurement, Logistics and Conversion. The team membership was representative of the company's structure, with staff members from many departments participating in areas formerly thought to be outside their areas of control. The teams were focused on a specific team charter, which outlined their aims and their goals.

An analysis of the materials and supplies used by the business showed that very many suppliers were involved in servicing the needs of Erin Foods. A further analysis of the stock levels of ingredients and packaging showed some ingredient stock levels well in excess of six months' worth of production. The procurement team moved to develop an understanding of what ingredients could be sourced from what suppliers. The team quickly identified the possibility of aggregating ingredients supply from a small core of high quality suppliers. Discussions were initiated with these potential suppliers, which ended with a major reduction in the number of suppliers and better purchasing terms.

The team also worked closely with the sales and marketing team and the product development team in an effort to minimise variations in packaging and also to find ways of developing a core set of ingredients.

Results Achieved

Significant savings have been realised in the area of working capital, where the focus has been on:

- Identifying key products and ingredients
- Reducing unnecessary multiplicity of packaging materials.
- Improving and developing supplier relationships and the supply of materials.

Overall, savings of more than €1.25 million have been achieved to date.

QUICKER, BETTER, CHEAPER ...
TOGETHER

The pressure is on for business to perform at higher levels of ability. The choices made as to how a business is organised will affect fundamentally its ability to deliver. If a business is set up, structured and resourced to make one type of product, then it will be very difficult to change to another product. For example, a fine chemical or pharmaceutical plant is usually built to produce a single product. The old-style car assembly plants were also difficult to change and inflexible, designed and built to make one type of vehicle.

The latest designs of car plants are designed from the outset for flexibility. Mitsubishi and Volvo have a joint venture manufacturing plant in Europe, where the Carisma and Volvo S40 cars are made in the same factory on the same assembly line, one after the other. One car can be a Volvo, the next a Volvo or a Mitsubishi – the system is designed to accommodate either. The strategic decision to build in flexibility to their designs for the factory meant that a number of basic design criteria for the cars had to be met – in particular, weld lines where the body sheets are joined had to be the same to facilitate robotic welding. The rest of the cars were specific to Volvo or Mitsubishi.

If one thinks creatively when arranging facilities, offices, manufacturing, or design departments and materials stores, one can find ways to build in flexibility, to remove time wastage and to ensure delivery of a quality service or manufacture of quality products.

Identifying which are good suppliers, who has the potential and the will to grow and who is willing to tackle inter-business wastes, is a major start toward to securing increased competitiveness.

Case Study: Neesons

Neeson's, a furniture manufacturer in Monaghan, bought its timber from a Danish supplier. As the machinists worked on the wood, they would often hit a knot in the timber and it would crack. Operators had been taking the cracked piece out of the machine and working on a new piece.

When the company introduced check sheets and run charts to the process, it identified the extent of the problem, gathered their facts and addressed their concerns to the supplier. Within weeks, the problem disappeared.

GETTING CLOSE

The demands of the market place mean business needs to be agile, responsive, and quality conscious. In the early days of world class implementation, the supply chain stretched from the manufacturer to the supplier, as in **Figure 72**.

FIGURE 72: SUPPLY CHAIN I

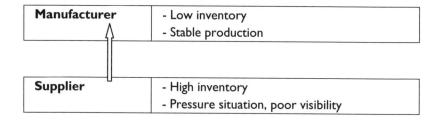

At that time, Just-in-Time meant that the big company held very little stock and demanded that their suppliers held it for them. The links with customers or end-users were often very poor. As the market changed, and the understanding of the possibilities of world-class practices developed, the importance of top class communication became clearer, as shown in **Figure 73**.

Developments in web technology and customer needs analysis tools led to the development of effective communication systems along the supply chain, as in **Figure 74**.

FIGURE 73: SUPPLY CHAIN 2

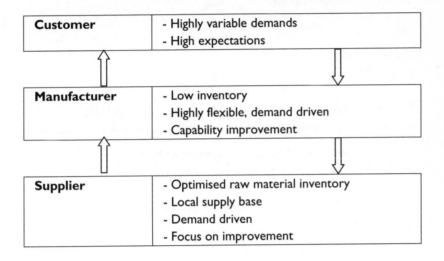

FIGURE 74: DATA LINKS ALONG THE SUPPLY CHAIN

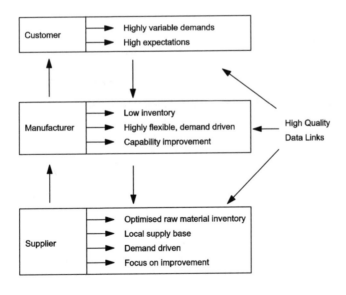

By focusing on building capability in both the manufacturer and the supplier, the levels of stock and the time to deliver to the customer can both be reduced. Below are two examples of companies that set out to meet their customers' needs.

Case Study:
COMPANY A

Company A decided to implement a very comprehensive MRP (Materials Requirement Planning) computer-based management system.

Management believed that such a system, when fully implemented and managed, would allow the company to service its customers' needs, based on forecasts and analysis. They invested heavily in computer equipment and staff training and became quite good at managing the MRP system.

However, their customers changed their minds about what products they wanted to buy. The company had not developed the processes that made the product, only how they managed the forecasting process and thus were unable to meet their customers' new needs.

Case Study:
COMPANY B

Company B decided to focus its efforts on building its ability to respond.

It trained staff in problem-solving techniques, quick change-over practices and the use of quality tools, developing their inherent capability.

When the customers changed their patterns of purchasing, Company B was able to follow them and continue to meet their needs.

These two examples show the basic difference in approach between companies adopting World Class Business techniques and those sticking with the traditional approach to business. One company builds the customer-focused ability of its people, while the other has built staff with good computer skills.

A balance needs to be struck between the use of computer systems and data transfer as aids to meeting customer needs and as internal management tools. Has a picture of the purchasing patterns of key customers been created? Do they have a purchasing pattern? If a pattern can be identified, it is often possible to communicate this to the customer to optimise the supply of materials along the supply chain. Some businesses are unaware of the impact of their purchasing patterns on their own businesses, let alone on others.

An example of two purchasing patterns are shown in **Figure 75**. The first pattern was the "normal" pattern of the customer: order a large quantity of product, use the product until it had run out and then pressure the supplier for rapid re-supply of another large quantity of stock.

FIGURE 75: PURCHASING PATTERNS

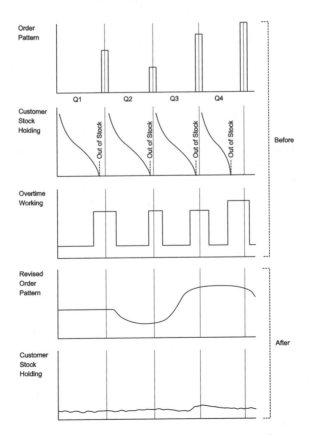

When stocks ran out, production of their own products was delayed, which led to increased overtime being worked after the deliveries were received. When the supplier mapped out this pattern of purchasing, a revised order pattern was developed, resulting in no stock shortages, reduced inventory costs and significantly reduced overtime charges, expedition charges and reduced pressure on the business.

Once again, do customers have a purchasing pattern? How can they be helped to see this pattern and to develop a new pattern that suits both supplier and customer businesses? The question of forecasting is addressed in **Chapter 14** and is a key element in the area of Communication along the supply chain.

STOCK ANALYSIS & MANAGEMENT

The most expensive component in any product is the one that is out of stock when it is needed. The real role of stock management is to ensure that parts and components are available to manufacturing or operations, as they are needed. The difficult balancing act of stock management is to achieve this objective with a minimum of stock holding.

The traditional approach to stock management has been to introduce paper- or computer-based stock control programmes. Stocks of parts are listed and checked and issued to production. The effectiveness of the system is dependent on the accuracy of paperwork within the system and the conscientiousness of all involved. For such systems to be reliable, accuracy levels of over 95% are required.

Each of these stock checks and paper transactions adds cost to the part, but no value. The focus in a world class plant is to find ways to maximise the value, while minimising the cost and providing effective management to the business.

For example, on recent visit by one of the authors to Subaru Cars in Japan, the number of exhaust manifolds sitting beside the assembly line was counted. A quick mental calculation, based on their daily throughput of cars, suggested that they had only two hours' worth of exhaust manifolds at the line. There was another two hours' worth in stores. This is in stark contrast to Western manufacturers, where days – if not weeks' – worth of parts and components are kept in store. A visit to Scania Trucks a number of years ago showed that they had invested heavily in installing a fully automated storage and retrieval system for completed engines, giving them a weeks' stock.

By the way, the calculations made in Subaru were wrong. The type of engine in the Subaru is known as a boxer engine, a horizontally-opposed flat-four engine, in which two exhaust manifolds are used per car. So Subaru was only stocking one hour's worth of manifolds! Their suppliers were delivering manifolds continually during each day.

Practical Stock Management – ABC Analysis

To reduce the cost of stocking parts, one needs to understand how the cost is made up. Not all parts are equally costly, not all parts are used in the same volume. Before one can decide on the best management policy for parts, one need to know which parts must be managed. ABC analysis can help in this regard.

The process starts with a listing of the parts in stores. This list is augmented with the annual usage levels and component unit price. Annual usage value is then calculated.

$$\text{Annual Usage Value} = \text{Annual Usage} \times \text{Unit Cost}$$

The list of components is then sorted by Annual Usage Value. Based on the Pareto principle, approximately 20% of the components will be responsible for 80% of the annual spend. This first 20% of parts are the "A" class items.

The A class items need to be managed aggressively. If possible, they should be located in a special area of the stores or, better still, where this is feasible, directly at the point of usage. In any case, the gathering of the A class items into one area helps focus attention on these costly items. Every effort should be made to develop supplier relationships to minimise the level of stocks that need to be maintained. In many cases, suppliers can accommodate requirements for more frequent deliveries if asked, and also if they are given some visibility on annual usage levels.

The focus of attention on parts usage should also extend to looking at suppliers for components. Are there many suppliers for the same part? Is there a good, still valid reason for this? Or is it just the way things are? Quite often, such purchasing patterns develop over time. The ABC analysis process can highlight these issues and possibly provide an opportunity to rationalise the supplier list, aggregate purchases with a core of suppliers and thus achieve improved terms of business.

"B" class items can also be identified from the Annual Usage Value list – usually, they account for 15% or so of annual purchases. These parts warrant less management input and can most readily be managed on, say, a two-weekly or monthly Kanban system.

"C" class items usually account for the last 5% of the annual usage and are the least important, from a financial point of view. However, the smallest, cheapest component of a machine can be the most costly, especially if it is out of stock. C class items do need to be managed aggressively – a Kanban of three months' usage levels will ensure sufficient parts are held in stock with minimal management input.

The availability of components to production in an efficient manner should be the objective of materials procurement staff. This can best be achieved through the development of both internal systems and a well-tuned, committed and capable supply chain.

WORLD CLASS CLUSTERS – COMPANIES WORKING TOGETHER

There is strength in unity. Small and medium-sized companies have certain advantages and disadvantages when compared to large, multi-national type companies:

Advantages	Disadvantages
Flexible	Short of people
Quick to move	Dependent on key
Short lines of	player
communication	Small scale
	Limited scope

Imagine if a number of SMEs were to align themselves into a virtual organisation, where their respective strengths would work together to build scale, address the people shortages and make the whole virtual organisation less dependent on individuals.

This approach is followed in a number of leading industrial areas of the world, most notably in Emilia Romagna in North Eastern Italy, home to such companies as Ferrari, Lamborghini and Ducati. In Emilia Romagna, clusters of SMEs co-operate to produce quality products. For example, in the furniture sector, four to eight companies work together to produce the elements of furniture with individual companies specialising in legs or seat-tops or table-tops. By specialising, they can develop true ability and expertise, and by co-operating they can produce products to world class standards, competitively.

This approach is dependent on high levels of communication and trust between companies. The linking of companies in this way ensures the mobility of small companies, the retention of their key advantages and the creation of the "virtual scale" necessary to facilitate competition in the international market place.

The application of World Class business techniques between companies clustering can lead to the identification and eradication of wastes. We have seen how these tools and techniques can do this within an individual business, but the opportunity also exists to develop an approach for Irish SMEs to apply World Class Business techniques in a cluster approach.

17: Innovation & Design

Most world class companies are trying to do two things simultaneously:

- Continuous improvements in existing products, services and systems, with the objective of getting better at what they are currently doing.
- Searching for a breakthrough, so as to enter new markets by developing new products, services or processes and to change their position in existing markets by doing different things from what they are currently doing.

The orientation of world class companies is to continuously "re-invent the company" – a form of accelerated Darwinian evolution of the company. Re-invention is a process of taking advantage of such environmental changes as markets, technology, political and changing lifestyles. Exploiting the new markets and the new opportunities as quickly as possible is a crucial success factor. The concept of "re-inventing the company" is at variance with the idea, which was popular in the 1980s, of creating and maintaining long-term competitive advantage – an unsustainable approach in the hyper-competitive 2000s.

Consider the following quotations:

> "Manufacturing must become a, if not *the*, primary marketing tool in the firm's arsenal. Quality, maintainability, responsiveness …. flexibility, and the length of the innovation cycle (for both incremental improvement of current products and major new product development) are all controlled by the factory."
> **Peters (1987)**

> "The factory is no longer a place of dirty floors and smoking machines, but rather an environment of ongoing experimentation and continuous innovation."
> **Kenney and Florida (1993)**

INNOVATION

Research workers use resources in seeking fundamental knowledge and understanding of "what is", whereas development workers use resources and research findings to create for the market "what never has been". Innovation is closer to development work than to research work, is generally associated with wealth creation, and may be considered as:

- New Product / Service Development
- Process Development
- Management Practices Development
- Business Model Development.

New Product / Service Development and Process Development will be considered below in the section on Design.

Management Practices Development is concerned with the development and adaptation of different management practices with a view to increasing the overall productivity of the organisation. The use of soft skills can have a profound impact on competitiveness. Soft skills here include methods of organisation, methods of working, managerial philosophy, leadership style, communications and supplier relationships. The objective for the organisation is to work better or more effectively rather than more intensively.

Business Model Development is innovation in relation to the manner the company conducts its business. With the advent of e-business, in its different forms, companies now have the opportunities of creating and serving global markets in ways that were not available some years ago. It is now possible to consider the development of "virtual organisations" to service specific markets and to form temporary alliances for some projects with organisations with whom one is competing with in respect of other projects.

Kanter (1991) offered the following six rules to inhibit innovation:

- Be suspicious of any new idea from below. After all, top management thinks of all the good ideas.
- Make people go through several organizational levels before getting your approval.
- Give criticism at every opportunity.
- Keep people in the dark about what's going on in the firm.
- Manage tightly; control everything to the nth degree.

- Have the attitude that you (top management) already know everything there is to know.

How many of these rules operate in your business?

Case Study:
De Bruin Iasc Teoranta

Ted Browne processes fish. Such a simple statement fails to capture the mastery and skill of a true craftsman. Ted and his team of people process salmon, prawns and crabs outside Dingle, in Co Kerry. Ted trained as a fisherman, a chef and a businessman. His love of food, and his meticulous attention to detail in the process chain, means that his salmon, prawn and crab products rank among the best there are.

Over the years, he has developed close links with the local fishermen to ensure the quality of his raw materials is optimised from the minute it leaves the water. The majority of his team's output is sold to high-end restaurants along the west coast of Ireland and in selected overseas markets.

Key Issues
Processing fish leaves significant wastes. To grow the business, one must address these wastes in a sustainable and effective manner. The company knew the waste was rich in potentially useful elements and minerals.

Response
The company analysed fully the content of its wastes and determined that there was, indeed, useful content in it. The challenge facing them was to convert this waste product into a by-product – to change a cost into a potential income stream. Working with leading research groups, they developed an innovative and effective process to compost the waste to produce a high quality horticultural compost product.

DESIGN

New Product / Service Development

A basic purpose of any business organisation is to provide goods and/or services to satisfy the requirements of its customers. Customers may independently specify their requirements and/or may be conditioned/educated to request certain characteristics of goods and/or services provided by the organisation. The requirements of customers are fundamental inputs to strategy formulation for the organisation. New product development (NPD) is often considered to be an essential ingredient for the long-term survival of a business. Some may even consider NPD to be the *raison d'être* of a business.

> "… Many elite Japanese companies embarked on an orgy of product proliferation during the 1980s. Sony, for example, introduced 300 versions of its basic Walkman (disclaiming the need for market research, it simply introduced a new model and saw how it sold) and Seiko was renowned for its ability to introduce a new watch model every working day."
> **Hayes and Pisano (1994)**

Design can confer competitive advantage on any organisation. Fundamentally, there are just two modes of competition: cost leadership or product/service differentiation. Appropriate design is a key to superior performance, no matter which mode of competition the organisation follows.

One can distinguish three types of design:

- **Product Design**, which is concerned with the specification at an appropriate level of all the physical aspects of the product, including, for example, the materials to be used, dimensions and tolerances required, components and other parts required, performance and safety standards of the product and individual components and the physical form, appearance and shape of the final product. In summary, product design is an integration of classical engineering design with industrial design.
- **Service Design**, which is concerned with the specification of the physical items, together with the sensual and psychological benefits the customer receives from the service experience.

- **Process Design**, which is concerned with the specification of the processes by which the product is produced or the service delivered. Usually, in the case of the production of products, process design specifies manpower, energy and machine requirements, as well as the sequence of processes involved. In respect of the provision of services, the customer is often an integral part of the service provided and so process design, in this case, must also consider issues relating to the convenience and comfort of the customer, the demeanour and approach of the server and the physical environment in which the service is delivered.

There is a very close relationship between good design of a product or service and the perceived quality of that product or service. Quality is essentially concerned with meeting or exceeding customers' expectations. The design function defines an organisation more clearly than other functions, in that it builds on the core competencies of the organisation and exposes gaps where new competencies must be established. Uniquely, design simultaneously specifies the customers of the organisation as well as the competitors of the organisation. Good design should therefore achieve:

- A close match between product/service offerings and customer requirements.
- A cost-effective and timely achievement of these requirements.
- A process that leads to ease of production of product or delivery of service.

In addition, speed of delivery of completed designs of new products or services is a very significant competitive advantage. A study undertaken by McKinsey & Co found:

- A 50% overrun in development costs affects profits by 3.5%.
- Product costs that are 9% too high have a 22% impact on profitability.
- Shipping a product to market six months too late leads to a 33% deterioration in total profits.

Although this study was concerned with high-volume, high-technology products, the key point is that design has a very serious impact on an organisation's profitability.

Design as a Process rather than a Function

Broadly speaking, business organizations are in existence to create, make and market products and/or services. Many organizations, and particularly SMEs, however, tend to be involved in either mainly the production of products or mainly the delivery of a service, but not usually both.

Although there is a degree of commonality between the design of a product and of a service, there are some differences in emphasis. For the sake of clarity, the following discussion will concentrate on the design of products.

World Class organisations have, over the last decade or so, realised that product design and innovation is too important for the success of the organisation to be left in the hands of traditionally-focused engineering departments. Design is now more and more considered to be a process requiring inputs from many departments, including marketing, engineering, cost accounting, purchasing and production/ manufacturing. Henry Ford's dictum that the "customer can have any colour provided it was black" would find little support in today's marketplace. Nevertheless, it was a very insightful view at the time and made possible the production of cars for the mass market.

The design process begins with ideas for new or improved products. The sources for these ideas are many, including the organisation's own staff, marketing research, customer complaints and suggestions, suppliers, new products developed by competitors, developments in new technology and products designed for markets other than one's usual markets. Cultivating an "innovative outlook" within an organisation is a characteristic of World Class business. To develop such a culture, employees must feel valued and be encouraged to express their views and make suggestions for improvements. Tolerance of failure, to some degree at least, is an essential element in the development of such a culture. Not all suggestions or ideas for innovation or new products will be fruitful, but the cost of missing out on the one that would be fruitful could be very high. Needless to say, a balance must be struck between the resources devoted to innovation and new idea generation and the normal expected day-to-day work of the organisation.

Given the business paradigm of Create – Make – Market – Assess, or the analagous Plan – Do – Check – Act cycle (PDCA-Deming Wheel) for continuous improvement, it is clear that product design is a multi-disciplinary process.

FIGURE 76: PDCA CYCLE

ASSESS	CREATE		ACT	PLAN
Information from Market Place	Idea Generation Design of Product		Full implementation Continue the improvement cycle	Problem Identification and Plan for Improvement
MARKET	MAKE		CHECK/STUDY	DO
Sales	Manufacture Buy in Parts		Results of Implementation	Implementation on a pilot basis

CMMA Cycle
Produce Cycle

PDCA Cycle
The Deming Wheel

However, in addition to being multi-disciplinary, best practice in design is that the disciplines/departments work together on the design concurrently, and not sequentially, or "over the wall", as tended to be the practice in the past. Concurrent design/simultaneous engineering is a prerequisite for reducing the time-to-market of new products.

It is well-known that failure rates in new product development and introductions to the market are high, but these rates may be reduced by a company-wide multi-functional, rather than a single-function, approach to new product innovation. New product development is a key opportunity for organisational learning, either through the development of technology or by forming alliances with other companies.

FIGURE 77: DEPARTMENTAL WALLS

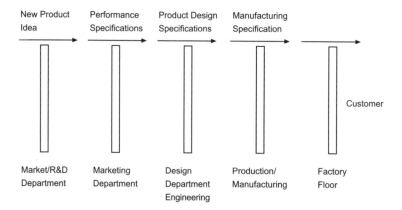

New Product Idea	Performance Specifications	Product Design Specifications	Manufacturing Specification		
					Customer
Market/R&D Department	Marketing Department	Design Department Engineering	Production/ Manufacturing	Factory Floor	

FIGURE 78: MULTI-FUNCTIONAL TEAMS

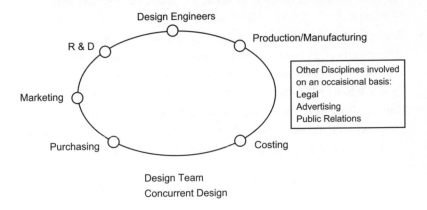

Design Team
Concurrent Design

The advantage of using multi-disciplinary design teams in a concurrent fashion are two-fold: cost and speed. Any required changes in the design of a product become much more costly the closer the product is to manufacture. If a product design has to be changed during manufacture (resulting in Engineering Change Orders, ECOs), the cost can be very high and might have been avoided, or reduced substantially, if manufacturing personnel had been involved with the design at an earlier stage. Likewise, it is important that marketing stay with the design team until production, and even after production, to ensure that customers' requirements are met.

There are clear quality advantages in manufacturing being involved with the design from the beginning because, as is well-known, quality thrives in a stable environment, from an operations viewpoint. The fewer ECOs the better from the point of view of operations, once production starts.

Techniques that may be of benefit in developing ideas for new products include:

- **Brainstorming,** which is a group technique for the identification and solution of problems. It is essential to have free expression of ideas and no criticism of any idea presented. Ideas are evaluated only *after* the completion of the brainstorming session. Brainstorming may be used in other areas, including quality improvement and process change.

- **Benchmarking,** itself, is clearly a source of new product ideas. Finding the best in class product or process and measuring the performance of the organisation against such standards is often a very important source of new ideas for products, services and processes.

- **Perceptual Maps** are visual displays comparing customer perceptions of different products (**Figure 79** presents a Perceptual Map of a particular size of tyre in a specified price range. There is clearly a market in this price range for a good grip, good wear tyre!).

- **Reverse Engineering** involves carefully dismantling and inspecting the products of competitors to assess design features. Such features can be adapted or enhanced, thus avoiding any patent infringement.

FIGURE 79: DESIGN PERCEPTUAL MAPS

Good Grip

Brand A

Good Wear   Poor Wear

Brand B   Brand C

Poor Grip

Very few SMEs can afford the costs and risks associated with large R&D departments. Ideas generated by R & D Departments often follow a very long path to commercialisation. Moreover, only about 5% of ideas for products are translated into actual products in the market place.

SMEs can use consultancy help from outside organisations. However, to obtain full benefit from such assistance, the SME must remain involved with the outside consultant and there should be a very clear focus on what is expected from the consultant. Institutes of Technology and Universities may be of assistance in some aspects of design but, again, such assistance must be managed properly for maximum benefit. Remember that whereas the consultant receives the fee, the company takes the risk in the market place.

Once the idea for a new product has been generated, the design process can commence. There are distinct phases in the design process as indicated in **Figure 80**.

FIGURE 80: DESIGN PROCESS PHASES

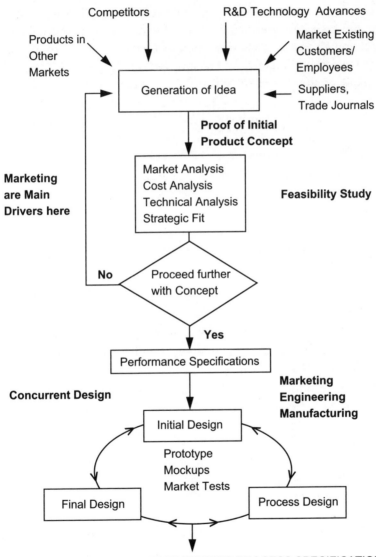

In the Feasibility Study, or Proof of Initial Product Concept, phase, alternative product concepts are evaluated using some form of market research such as customer surveys, focus groups, interviews and discussions with experienced sales personnel. Should there be a perceived demand for the new product, then initial cost analysis should be undertaken.

Technologies such as break-even analysis, decision theory, discounted cash flow are sometimes used to evaluate the profitability of producing the product. Data used in most cost analyses are probabilistic rather than certain in nature and so any such analysis should include an assessment of the risk involved and, consequently, the organisation's attitude to risk. Associated with the cost analysis, there is a need to consider technical and strategic issues relating to the proposed new product.

The following questions must be answered:

- Does the organisation have the managerial and technical skill required to manage the new product project and actually produce the product?
- Are there any capital resources requirements that the organisation may have difficulty in funding?
- Is the overall risk excessive?
- What about available or unused capacity in the manufacturing and warehousing areas?
- Are there likely to be any supplier problems?
- Is there a good strategic fit with other products currently being manufactured?
- Is the new product compatible with the core business of the company and will it provide competitive advantage?

Clearly, the input of top management is very desirable, before it is decided to proceed with the design of the product. Arising out of the Feasibility Study, performance specifications for the new product can be developed, describing what the product should do to satisfy customer requirements.

Once this stage is reached, the philosophy of full concurrent design comes into play. The performance specifications are translated into technical specifications of the physical product. An initial design is developed, a prototype is produced, the prototype is tested and a further design is developed. The sequence of design – build a prototype – test –

redesign – may be repeated a number of times until the design team is satisfied.

Note that product design includes both Form Design and Function Design:

- **Form Design** is concerned with the physical appearance of the product, shape, colour, size and style. Image, personal identification and market appeal are all part of form design. Form design may be very important in consumer products – for example, mobile phones, cars – but less so in industrial products – for example, motor generator sets.

- **Function Design** is concerned with how the product performs. In some products Form Design usually takes precedence over Function Design. However, it is Function Design that ensures the product's fitness for use by the customer. Two important criteria of Function Design are the reliability and maintainability of the product after manufacture.

The Process Design goes hand in hand with the Product Design, and the whole design process is one of iteration to an end position of Final Product Design and Final Process Design, both of which are taken over by Manufacturing for implementation.

World class organizations are assisted during the design process by the use of techniques such as Quality Function Deployment (QFD), CAD/CAM, Computer Aided Process Planning (CAPP), Failure Mode Effects Analysis (FMEA), Fault Tree Analysis (FTA) and Value Analysis (VA).

Design teams should keep in mind the need to protect the company against product liability claims. The best defence against such claims are design reviews with a comprehensive and defendable trail of state-of-the-art design decisions taken in respect of the product.

After the production process has settled down, various quality assurance techniques are required to optimise quality objectives.

The following causes of design failures, listed by Hutchins (1988), indicate the need for designers to be very conscious of attending to detail:

- Incorrect materials
- Vague/ambiguous specifications for materials, treatments, etc.
- Inadequate allowance for fatigue/strength loss over the specified life of the product

- Not allowing for environmental factors, including dirt, fumes, etc.
- Poor design for manufacture – including ease of manufacture and low cost
- Inadequate user and installation instructions.

We now look at a number of specific elements of design that can contribute significantly to both cost and quality of delivered product, in a simple way, including:

- Simultaneous Design
- Design for Manufacture
- Modularity
- Standardisation
- Part Count
- Design for Assembly
- Design for Testing
- Design for Process
- Product Evaluation.

Simultaneous Development

Simultaneous development can work where communication levels are good. The traditional design process results in sequential development. Designs are completed before packaging work starts, before production processes are designed, before materials are sourced, etc. This results in a build-up of lead-times, as each downstream department has its own lead-time requirements to complete the specific stages of the new product introduction process.

By ensuring that communication levels are good, individual team members can make decisions early and well that short-circuit the overall product introduction cycle. Design and Marketing need to work closely together so that designers truly understand the needs and desires of the end-users. As this closeness develops, a company's products are more closely attuned to the requirements of the market place and so are more likely to be bought.

Design for Manufacture

A well-designed product with lots of marketable features that cannot be manufactured effectively is a poorly-designed product.

A company designs products to satisfy or exceed customers' needs and requirements. But the company also has needs and requirements – it needs to satisfy its stakeholders, it needs to make a profit, it needs to continue in business and develop. If the products it designs cannot be manufactured profitably, then it will fail.

Modularity

The design for manufacture concept works to help companies design products that can be manufactured effectively.

Back in the 1930s and 1940s, General Motors came to understand this concept. Very many of their models were designed using main modules that were then packaged in different outer skins. We see the same happening today, with SAAB offering GM engines in a number of models. By using well-proven designs but, using tried and tested modules, a company can significantly reduce a product's development time as well as reducing the complexity within the production area when it comes to time to manufacture the product.

Standardisation

If a company can standardise on a number of modules or sub-assemblies across its product range, significant savings can be made at the production level.

Designers want to design – it is, after all, their basic function – but their creative talents are best used when they design using standardised components or parts. The range of parts available today means that any number of designers can design a product to meet a given specification, without any two of them using the same components from the same source. It is fundamentally important to put some basic controls on the type and variety of components available for choice by the design team.

Part Count

The number of parts required to make up a product is a very important consideration when it comes to manufacture.

The electronics industry has been a front-runner in this quest for Part Count Reduction. By reducing the number of parts, one:

- Reduces inventory
- Reduces handling
- Reduces the number suppliers

- Improves quality.

The fewer the number of parts, the better the quality opportunity.

Design for Assembly

The previous point of reducing part count has an equally important application in the area of design for assembly. By reducing the number of parts, the labour content of the assembly operation can be reduced.

By designing products with a view to how they will be assembled in production, designers can have a significant impact on manufacturability – for example, useful techniques to improve production performance include:

- Ensuring products can be assembled from the bottom up, avoiding the necessity to turn them over for access.
- Minimising the number of parts, of bolted joints, of replacing bolted assemblies with snap fits, of improving alignment systems.

Fool-proofing at the assembly stage can save large amounts of lost time and waste further along the assembly line. Design products so there is only one, obvious way to assemble them.

Design for Testing

The test function is quite often a bottleneck in a manufacturing operation. Parts or covers need to be removed, test points are difficult to get at or new, unproven sub-assemblies or components have been incorporated in a design thus requiring extensive testing of products in an effort to ensure product quality is not compromised. Designers should design to allow for quick and effective testing.

Design for Process

Simplicity has been a constant thread running through the tools and techniques of WCB.

When designing a new product, consideration should be given to how it will be manufactured, to the physical processes required to get it made. Unless specific technological requirements demand it, it is best to stick to tried and proven processes. Proven equipment can manufacture with a degree of consistency not always obtainable from new age technologies.

Frequently, the winning companies let a technology pass the experimental and first-rush stages before incorporating it as an integral element of their core production processes.

Product Evaluation

It is important to know what is happening in your market. When a new product is launched by competitors, it is very important that your staff get as good understanding of it as soon as possible. In Europe, each of the main truck manufacturers issue their sales staff with competitive analyses of their competitors' products.

Close scrutiny of competitors' products can pay dividends for your company. You may see a new idea that, when modified or developed by your own staff, may lead to significant improvements and cost savings. The product evaluation process should be organised and professionally carried out. Ideally, your own customers' requirements analysis should be used when examining competitive products, to see where the competition rests in relation to your own features and characteristics:

- By critically examining the features of competitive products you can ascertain how well your own product meets the customers requirements.

- When sales volumes are factored into the analysis you can come to an understanding of the sensitivity of the market to different factors and features.

- A simple analysis of what the customer places emphasis on could be a starting point for a re-examination of the interpretation of the customers' buying criteria, and possibly of product positioning in the market.

CONCLUSION

A well-designed product will perform as intended, will have high reliability, will be easy and economical to maintain, will be safe and environmentally-friendly in use and will be easily and safely made at low cost, relatively speaking.

The following quotation aptly summarises the central concept of this chapter:

> "At the core of the new model of innovation-mediated production stands a set of fundamental changes in the

organization of work at the point of production – a "new shop floor" – which is geared toward harnessing and mobilizing intellectual labour. Both the factory floor and the R&D laboratory become a source of continuous innovation, productivity improvement, value creation, and capital accumulation."

Kenney and Florida (1993)

18: ABC & Strategy –
Bringing It All Together

Many books on business development start with strategy. They say that a business needs a strategy before it can develop. The ABC approach is different. It is based on the fact that most businesses already have product offerings, assets and customers, its strategy is largely a given and so ABC is focused on helping identify ways to meet and exceed competition levels within a sector by adopting good business practice. But there is still a definite need for strategy within a business applying ABC.

Business strategy can be likened to map reading. Before a map can be used effectively, it is essential to know the starting point, the destination and to be able to see the map and understand it, and to be able to work out a route. Business strategy provides the map for a business. By clearly identifying the starting point, say, using benchmarking as a diagnosis tool, and by stating an objective, the business strategy can help to rally the efforts of all involved in a business to achieve that goal. If the strategic objectives of the business are not clearly stated, if they stay inside the heads of the management, then it is very difficult for others to know where the business is going and to work out how they are supposed to help get the business there.

A good strategic plan should include a Mission or Vision for the company which tells people the big picture.

GOALS

Goals are results or objectives that need to be to achieved. These need to be real and easily understood to act as clear targets for management and workers. As examples, these goals could be:

- To achieve x % percent profitability

- To make sales of €y per year
- To be integrated into the local community.

An effective strategic plan needs to look internally at the company itself and externally at its customers, its competitors and the community or environment within which it operates (see **Figure 81**).

FIGURE 81: STRATEGY

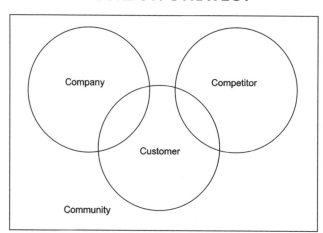

CUSTOMERS

A business exists to meet the needs of its clients or customers. To do this effectively, it must know and understand those needs. It must understand the difference between customers' needs and customers' wants. It needs to know who the customers are, what they buy, how often and in what quantities and varieties. It is important to understand why customers do business with the company rather than with its competitors. It is also important to have an understanding of how important individual customers are to the business. It is not enough to rank customers in terms of volume of sales – they should also be ranked in terms of profitability potential for growth and ease of doing business.

Often, a customer list has grown organically over time. The list may have a combination of low-value, high-maintenance customers as well as low-maintenance, high-value customers. The challenge for management, when preparing a strategic development plan for the business, is to maximise the benefit for the business from the customer base. This can often involve a re-examination of the customer base with a move to re-focus sales efforts. By ranking customers using A, B, C analysis (see **Chapter 14**), we can often bring clarity to the sales function with improved overall benefit for the business.

Case Study: Kent Stainless

Based in Wexford, the company is a leading designer and manufacturer of stainless steel products. It was started in 1982 by Pat Kent, with five people. In the late 1990s, Pat Kent was faced with the choice of growing his business or deciding to remain small. He chose growth.

Strategy within Kents
The company started its growth phase by looking at its internal capabilities, in particular, its management team, its manufacturing resources and the skills of its workforce. It also examined its customer profile, looking at market opportunities, product-market alignment and customer appropriateness.

It quickly identified the need to re-focus the business on growth markets and to augment the management team, by looking for a senior executive who had:
• Overseas sales and marketing expertise.
• Experience of growing business.
• Strong team development capabilities.

The company located such a person, and moved onwards to identify and develop strong sales and marketing strategies. It now sells widely overseas in such key areas as the Far East and Europe.

The company:
• Segregated the business into specific business units.
• Rationalised the customer base.
• Focused on key markets and opportunities where its skills and capabilities are rewarded.
• Identified upstream opportunities, acquiring a waste processing machine business where its drainage products form a natural alliance.

The company continues to grow organically and by acquisition, focused on an appropriate combination of market needs and inherent capabilities.

COMPETITION

There are very few businesses that function without competition. If competitors exist, it is important to be aware of who they are, what they are good at, what their products are and what features and weaknesses they exhibit. Effectively, competitors are trying to take business away and a business needs to defend itself from them.

Learn about and study competitive products. The examination of other people's solutions can often act as a stimulus to your own creativity, resulting in improved designs and increased customer satisfaction. Much of engineering advance over the years has been based on learning from others and innovating.

COMPANY

You must "know yourself". When working on a strategy, take the time to determine objectively the business' strengths and weaknesses. If people do not know what their business is capable of, then they may well set themselves unrealistic (too high or too low) targets and objectives. If they do not identify weaknesses at all, they may expose the business to failure or un-sustainable stress.

The benchmarking process can help in identifying clearly and objectively the strengths and weaknesses of the business when compared to its sector and beyond. The SWOT technique, which is discussed shortly, provides a useful tool to assist in this process of self-identification.

COMMUNITY

Businesses operate within a Community. They are affected by that community's laws and regulations. Similarly, the community laws can provide opportunities for business. It is important that a business consider future changes in legislation, changes in demographics that may affect it as well as changes in technology as they move to develop their future strategy.

A number of tools have been developed to help companies understand their businesses and to help formulate a strategic plan.

SWOT ANALYSIS

A SWOT analysis looks at the Strengths, Weaknesses, Opportunities and Threats facing a business.

SWOT analysis looks at the internal and external environment facing a business. On the internal front, the technique looks at the Strengths of the business, seeking to reinforce them and to identify potential strategic advantage for the company. By identifying Weaknesses, a business team can work to fix them, to find improvement to reduce their weaknesses.

On the external side, the company focuses on the Opportunities that may exist, with a view to focusing on them and exploiting them as a concerted team. The team can identify Threats to their business and move to take counter-measures to protect the business.

A flipchart can be useful when doing a SWOT analysis, as it provides a highly visual way of capturing information. The usual way of representing the data is presented in **Figure 82**.

FIGURE 82: SWOT

As the team examine their business, their customers, and their competition using the SWOT technique, real plans can be developed to make the business stronger.

PRODUCT-MARKET MATRIX

We have so far looked at customers, the company itself and the competition. The product-market matrix tool looks at the full product range of a business, with a view to clearly identifying which products have potential for growth and which are in decline. The tool uses a box system (see **Figure 86**), with all products are located on the matrix. The use of this visual approach often helps a full business team to plan actions to maximise returns in the short to medium term or to identify the need to develop new products lines or innovations to secure the business into the future.

FIGURE 83: PRODUCT-MARKET MATRIX

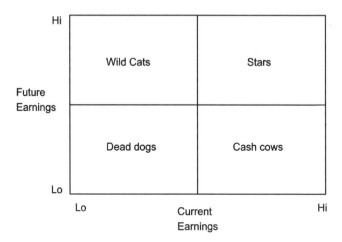

The tool uses the following classifications to characterise products. Each classification leads to its own strategic plan.

- **Wild Cats:** Products with the potential to deliver high future earnings. Often unproven and maybe needing further development.

- **Dead Dogs:** Providing low present and future earnings potential. These may be "bread and butter" products and would be unlikely to receive much investment.
- **Cash Cows:** Proven products with a limited life horizon. The strategy here is to maximise revenue with limited investment. Get as much from the product as possible.
- **Stars:** Proven current high earners with high potential future earnings. Significant investment would be made to maximise the life contribution of these products.

When a business uses the product-market matrix tool, it can usually identify where it should be focussing sales and marketing efforts, as well as their manufacturing and innovation time.

The use of the tool can also be helpful in bringing attention to the life cycle of particular products or offerings. If there are no new products planned for the future, this fact can be clearly identified and action taken in time.

Bringing It All Together

A business strategic plan provides the business with a clear direction for the future. It helps everybody involved with the business to understand how their efforts contribute to the overall goals and objectives of the operation.

Once the high level strategy has been defined, it is up to individual elements of the business to develop their strategies. Sales and Marketing, Design and Operations as well as Finance all need to develop their individual strategies to deliver on the overall business strategy. In actual fact, this is an interactive process. The business strategy needs to be based on the abilities and resources of the business, and *vice versa*.

The business strategy provides a rallying call to ensure that all members of the business are working towards a common goal. Good implementation of a good strategy leads to good results.

19: IMPLEMENTATION

The general in-company approach followed for World Class implementation is represented graphically in **Figure 84**.

FIGURE 84: HIGH INTENSITY WORLD CLASS IN-COMPANY IMPLEMENTATION MODEL

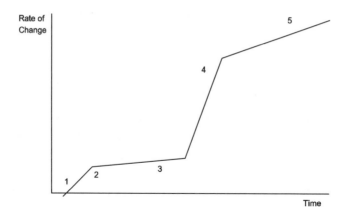

The approach consists of:

1. Business Diagnostic
2. World Class Business (WCB) - Awareness and Self Assessment
3. Implementation Planning
4. Step Changes
5. Continuous Improvement.

The approach is roughly based on Shewhart (1938, 1969) and the Lucas Business Systems approach (1991). It can be described as being the first five steps up an improvement ladder or stairs. From an overall perspective, the approach is best described as the first coil of an improvement spiral, rather than an improvement circle.

STEP 1: BUSINESS DIAGNOSTIC

"Before moving to a new land it is advisable to know where you are starting from".

The business diagnostic involves a review of key areas of the business: Finance, Marketing, Selling, Materials, Management Structure, R&D and in particular, Operations.

The main objective of this phase is to identify problems facing the business. This review of the current business situation can yield new insights into the nature of its problems. Some shortcomings in the manner in which the business is managed may come to light at this stage. Sometimes early actions or "quick hits" can achieve disproportionate gains, winning credibility for the team and management commitment for the more intensive improvement drive yet to come.

The starting point can be a simple benchmarking exercise to identify issues or areas of difficulty facing the business. When starting on an improvement activity, it is best to focus people's efforts on tangible problems or issues. An analysis of the current sales profile can help identify key products or customers (**Chapter 15**). An analysis of the key processes can help identify priority areas for action.

STEP 2: WCB AWARENESS & SELF ASSESSMENT

WCB programmes are generally driven by the senior mangers of a business, which means that the senior managers must have a clear understanding of what WCB involves in order to pass on their knowledge to the rest of the workforce. The key individuals involved need to understand the main principles of WCB and, more importantly, appreciate how those principles can be best put to use in their own company.

Once the company has come to an understanding of these basic principles, it can compare the results of the diagnostic phase against these principles as a form of Self Assessment. This assessment can be used as a basis for the implementation plan for the company. This interpretation process of the basics of WCB will lead to the planning and implementation phase.

STEP 3: IMPLEMENTATION PLANNING

At this stage, the company has learned about WCB and interpreted these principles in relation to real issues within the company. The company diagnostic phase has identified a number of potential areas for improvement. The combination of these two elements allows the company to move to create an implementation plan.

A successful implementation plan needs to be practical and flexible. Practical improvements achieved at an early stage of the implementation programme will have a very positive effect on the morale of all concerned. The plan should be balanced between detail and flexibility. It is generally better to err on the side of flexibility at the planning stage, as this leaves the way open to get the best out of the full team, both at management and at worker level, as the process continues.

STEP 4: STEP CHANGE

At this juncture, the examination has taken place; the company has learnt about, and come to its own understanding of, WCB. Planning has also taken place and it is now time to implement the changes.

One of the features of WCM is that, at this point in the process, relatively minor changes begin taking place within the company. Generally, these changes arise from a concerted implementation push as the operation moves into a new gear.

This stage is generally the most exciting and interesting part of the WCB programme, as employees see major changes and generally major improvements. However, this is also the time when the process is most likely to go wrong. Because the company is moving through a process of serious change, the reaction of personnel to change must be carefully managed. It is at this point that the importance of the previous two steps – WCB awareness and implementation planning – really come home to the company.

STEP 5: CONTINUOUS IMPROVEMENT

The initial stages of a WCB programme will lead to a number of immediate improvements in the general operation of the company. It is important to remember, however, that the company will need to continue the improvement process into the future.

It is strongly recommended that the company prepare a plan at the outset of the programme, to provide for training and ongoing assessment, to ensure that the WCB principles become ingrained in the company.

WORLD CLASS NETWORK IN-COMPANY IMPLEMENTATION MODEL

A World Class Network approach has been developed by the authors in conjunction with Enterprise Ireland and is an evolutionary approach, developed as a practical response to the requirements and resources of SMEs.

The improvement model for this framework looks like a series of incremental improvement steps and involves ongoing diagnostic analysis and improvement project identification throughout the project. The process is presented diagrammatically in **Figure 85**.

The World Class Network approach is modelled on the Japanese Kaizen, or small improvement steps, method. This approach is represented in **Figure 86** as a movement up the steps of a staircase. At each step, a business needs to identify its current state of performance as well as the key issues facing it. As time progresses, the issues are likely to change. As a business grows, it has requirements and faces challenges that were not present when it was smaller. Managers and staff need to identify this evolution and address the "hierarchy of needs" of the business and work to create and develop the future business.

FIGURE 85: WORLD CLASS NETWORK IN-COMPANY IMPLEMENTATION MODEL

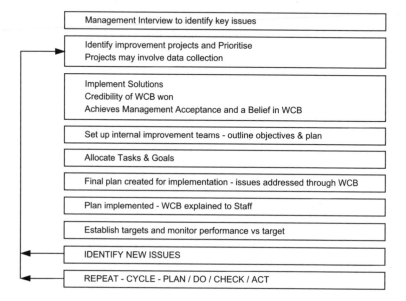

FIGURE 86: WORLD CLASS NETWORK IMPLEMENTATION MODEL – COMPANY LEVEL

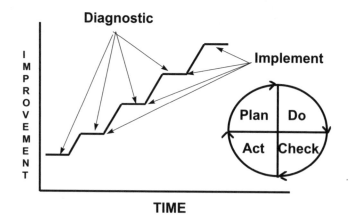

LEVEL 3

LEVEL 3

Process Benchmarking: Chapter 21	**The Five Ss: Chapter 22**	**Total Productive Maintenance: Chapter 23**	**Overall Equipment Efficiency: Chapter 24**
Six Sigma: Chapter 25	**Business Excellence: Chapter 26**	**Value Management, Analysis & Engineering: Chapter 27**	**Lean Production: Chapter 28**

Target Cost Management: Chapter 29

LEVEL 2

Facilitated Assessment benchmarking: Chapter 7 Saving Time: Chapter 10	Physical & Process Flow in the Office: Chapter 8 Maintenance: Chapter 11	Physical & Process Development: Chapter 8 Practical Quality: Chapter 12	Production Control Systems: Chapter 9 Teams & Team-Building: Chapter 13
World Class Sales: Chapter 14 ABC & Strategy: Chapter 18	Financial Management: Chapter 15 Implementation: Chapter 19	Supply Chain & Logistics: Chapter 16	Innovation & Design: Chapter 13

LEVEL 1

Self Assessment benchmarking: Chapter 5 Basic Maintenance: Chapter 5	Physical Flow: Chapter 5 Check Sheets: Chapter 5	Process Flow: Chapter 5 Run Charts: Chapter 5	Set-Up Time Reduction: Chapter 5 People & Teams: Chapter 6

20: "To Infinity & Beyond"[1]

The business has now mastered the fundamental tools and techniques of Levels 1 and 2. It is competing well at national level and has started to sell in the world market. So, what comes next?

By this point, both managers and staff should be aware that there are some really strong operators on the world stage. They should be aware that they have achieved significant improvements within their operations, through their own efforts. They should also be painfully aware that the real challenge has just begun. They will be running with the big dogs now! If they have successfully managed to reach Level 3, they will be willing and able to move to the next levels of challenge.

At Level 3, a business should be seeking to make Continuous Improvement a bedrock of the operation. Management and staff must realise that they have two jobs to do:

- The "day job"
- To find ways to improve the effectiveness of the operation.

Managers can realise real benefits for all by building this realisation and fostering the enthusiasm of all concerned with the business. This includes both suppliers and customers.

This section will not try to give comprehensive information on the more advanced World Class techniques. It will provide some insight into some of the more useful tools and techniques as a taster. In this way, managers will have the opportunity of considering which approach may help them in addressing the key strategic challenges facing their operations.

The section presents information on:

- Process Benchmarking
- The 5 S system
- Total Productive Maintenance (TPM)

---

[1]   Buzz Lightyear, *Toy Story*.

- Overall Equipment Efficiency
- Six Sigma
- Business Excellence Model
- Value Management, Analysis, Engineering
- Lean Production.

And finally, it is no surprise or coincidence that the best businesses in the world use or have used one or several of these approaches to achieve superior performance over the years.

Excellence is no accident, it is the result of strong leadership identifying a goal and harnessing the combined strengths and abilities of other people and the available assets to achieve that goal. By focusing people's attention on stretch targets, the world's best companies build their people through constant innovation. These tools and techniques support this effort. It is not magic – it is hard work – but it is rewarding for all.

21: Process Benchmarking

This is probably the most difficult type of benchmarking to do, although possibly the most beneficial, if it is done correctly.

Process benchmarking involves company staff in identifying a key issue for the business, mapping the internal process associated with that issue and identifying leading examples of how this process is handled in other businesses. These leading examples may be outside their own sector and in the private or public sectors. When leading organisations in the process have been identified, they are approached with a view to arranging a study mission.

The process benchmarking approach is often quite involved and can absorb significant amounts of time and money. The true benefit of process benchmarking is realised at the implementation stage, when improvements identified are implemented back in one's own company.

A business starting out on a process benchmarking exercise is focussing on achieving best practice within its operation. It wants, or needs, to be performing at the highest level. When looking for best practice, a benchmarking team is looking to identify a successful method to deliver a process. It is important to be sure that the method is proven to deliver results, it is not enough to look for a different method. If a benchmarked process is to be useful to a business, then it needs to be able to demonstrate clear benefits over the existing process.

However, it is very seldom that a process can be copied from one operation to another. Circumstances are often different – for example, interfacing processes and customer requirements can be different. It is essential to understand the fundamentals of the benchmarked process to enable effective adaptation of the process to meet specific business needs, without compromising the effectiveness of the benchmarked process.

HOW TO PROCESS BENCHMARK

The first, and possibly most important, step in process benchmarking is identifying *what process* to benchmark. It is essential to identify a process that is sufficiently significant to the sustainable competitiveness of a business that it warrants the dedication of resources to its improvement.

The second key step in the process is to identify *who* to benchmark with. It may seem ideal to benchmark your invoice processing with a world leading company, but maybe the scale and scope of such a business is too big. Think carefully to identify who has significantly better process performance. It is not always necessary to chase "best practice"; it can often be very sensible to look for "better practice" first, learning about and implementing that before chasing "best practice".

It is also worthwhile to think about how well the processes of others perform, to find measures of performance that can help you identify better and best practice operators.

A four-stage Process Benchmarking approach is presented in **Figure 87**, and described in the following sections.

FIGURE 87: PROCESS BENCHMARKING CYCLE

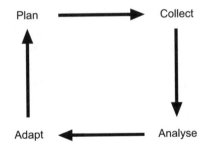

STAGE 1: PLAN

The first stage in a successful process benchmarking exercise is to plan the activity. This stage can be broken down into a number of elements:

1. **Form a benchmarking team:** Ideally, select people who have experience of improvement activities, and who have knowledge of using the tools presented in Levels 1 and 2.

2. **Document the selected process:** It is essential that the detail of the selected process is known and understood before going to examine other people's processes. The simple act of documenting the chosen process can lead to the identification of wastes and improvement opportunities. Fix these before going to look at other processes.

3. **Establish the scope of the study:** The project needs to be clearly defined and achievable. If the scope is too broad, then the project may well be impossible to complete.

4. **Define objectives for the process:** Set some targets that will challenge the team but that are likely to show a positive outcome for the effort.

5. **Develop criteria for benchmark partners:** Who would be appropriate to benchmark with? Should they be in the same sector, or country? What size of business is appropriate?

6. **Identify potential benchmark partners:** People often think this is very hard to do. Think clearly about who would be interesting, stimulating and rewarding to visit. A number of benchmarking clubs exist where those interested in benchmarking work together to improve their operations.

7. **Determine a data collection plan:** Identify some key measures and methods that will facilitate the collection of the right information to help understand the detail of the benchmarked processes. Work hard at this point, as careful identification of triangulated measures that can provide deep insights into good practice are very helpful. Try to find more than one measure for a practice, so that measures support or negate each other. If you find two independent measures that support each other, then it is likely that you have found good practice.

STAGE 2: COLLECT

It is now time to start collecting data on the potential benchmark partners. It is useful, and polite, to learn as much as possible about potential partners before contacting them. Careful preparation will make it clear that this benchmark process is both professional and well thought-out. Potential partners will appreciate that the groundwork has been done and that there is a logic to their selection for, and participation in, the process.

A number of distinct steps are involved:

1. **Carry out secondary research on the potential partners against the sort criteria:** What has been published about their operations or their processes? What is in the trade journals or business magazines? Is there academic research published about them?

2. **Evaluate the research and finalise the potential partners list:** Research sources can often be helpful in confirming potential partners or in deciding to remove them from the list. Work to finalise the potential partner list.

3. **Develop the data collection instrument:** The instrument or questionnaire must capture the basic information required to understand the practices, methods and techniques employed by the benchmark partners.

4. **Pilot the data collection instrument internally:** Use the questionnaire internally, before sending it to any potential partners. Check to ensure that all questions are understood without additional explanation. Also check that the answers given to questions are understood and clear. Adjust the questionnaire if necessary.

5. **Contact potential benchmark partners and enlist their participation:** The moment of truth. Potential partners must be contacted and enlisted to join the exercise.

6. **Carry out site visits:** Conduct a detailed site visit to the chosen partners. Use the questionnaire and also keep notes of discussions. Share the workload during the site visit between the team members. Remember, two pairs of eyes are better than one, so use time on site to maximum effect.

7. **Review site visit information:** After each visit, carry out a de-briefing session where each team member shares what they saw, heard and learned during the visit. Capture these insights. Also capture any outstanding questions that were not asked or answered during the visit or which arose following the de-briefing. Use telephone or email contact with the benchmark partner to address these questions.

STAGE 3: ANALYSE

Having captured the basic information, it is essential to see what can be learned from the data, to turn it into information and potential benefit.

The steps here are:

1. **Compare current in-house performance data to benchmark partners' data:** How does the internal operation compare with what was observed at the benchmark partners?

2. **Identify operational best practice and enablers:** Typically, there will be some aspects of each of the benchmark partners' processes that are worth noting. It is unusual to find one single source of best practice. List out what appears to be the best combination of practices. Look to find the best grouping from all the benchmarked sites, including your own. It is important to understand whether there are any fundamental factors that are critical to the adoption of best practice in the sites visited. If these cannot be replicated in your workplace, it may be impossible to transfer best practice.

3. **Develop an implementation plan and strategy:** What is to be implemented and how will it contribute to improving the core process? What level of resources or infrastructural change will be required to ensure the successful adaptation and adoption of best practice? Time spent at this stage of the process is often fundamental to assuring a successful outcome.

STEP 4: ADOPT

Now comes time to start implementing the improvements at base.

The steps are:

1. **Implement the plan:** Take action, being aware of difficulties that may be encountered and being quick to respond to them. If staff have problems, work with them to find positive solutions. If their problems are ignored, it could result in the failure of the exercise as staff revert to the old ways. Also, by addressing and understanding problems with implementation, it is often possible to develop even better and more effective responses to the process problems. Adaptation and innovation at this stage will often yield further improvements.

2. **Monitor and report progress:** People need to see that their efforts to improve are being recognised. By monitoring progress over time, it will be possible to show either improvements achieved or problems encountered. Either way, everyone will be aware that the process is important to the business and that their efforts are appreciated.

3. **Plan for Continuous Improvement:** When people have become comfortable with the new process, ask them where and how they think they can improve it further. This is particularly important for strategically significant processes. The simple act of asking whether the process can be improved further often yields results based on the accumulated experience of staff using the already improved process.

CONDUCTING A BENCHMARKING EXERCISE

We have presented above the mechanics of a benchmarking exercise. We now look at some of the softer aspects, including some basic considerations, how one might find benchmark partners, some general causes for failure and success and finishing with a checklist for conducting a successful exercise.

Basic Considerations

There are a number of basic considerations involved with a process benchmarking exercise. These can be classified generally as relating to the manners and practicalities.

The first of these points is Reciprocity. It should go without saying that, if another business opens its doors to your team, then you should be prepared to return the favour. So, one should be careful and aware of this when considering who to approach. Reciprocity usually also extends to the sharing of general results identified in the study. It is normal for the lead company to create a final report on the full exercise and to circulate it to all businesses involved in the exercise.

When trying to decide on benchmark partners, try to identify partners whose operations or processes are similar to your own. If the process or business is too dissimilar, then it can be very difficult to convince others back at base that there are lessons to be learned.

Be careful in what metrics are chosen to measure performance. Be sure to try them out in your own operation first. Remember, metrics can often be manipulated by capable managers. The story is told of the American factory that was reported to be making twice as many units per day as the Irish subsidiary, using the same process and manning levels per shift. This fact was accepted within the organisation, until it was realised that the US plant was running on a three-shift basis as opposed to the Irish two-shift operation.

The objective of a process benchmarking exercise is to gain a true and deep understanding of the benchmarked processes. If only a superficial knowledge is gained, it is very unlikely that any real insights will be gained and even less likely that any true value will be achieved.

Remember the benchmarking code of conduct. Do not look where you are not supposed to. Do not ask commercially sensitive questions. Do not risk compromising yourself or your business.

Causes of Failure and Success

Experience has shown that there are a number of causes that can lead to either a successful or a failed benchmarking exercise.

Causes of failure include:

- Own processes not properly documented
- Performance gap not identified
- Scope of project too big – broad *vs.* deep
- Not learning from what is available (renouncing the expert)
- Looking for best practice, when better practice may be a sufficient target
- Lack of management support
- Refusing to see and/or believe internal weaknesses or other's superior performance.

Causes of success include:

- Senior management as process owners
- Concept of Continuous Improvement in place
- The team understands the benchmarking process
- Timing is right – for the company and its benchmarking partners.

This section on process benchmarking concludes with a checklist for success:

- Project has top management commitment

- Project focuses on key business issues
- Project supports overall business improvement strategy
- Project demonstrates benefits outweigh costs
- Project allocates necessary human resources
- People involved have the necessary knowledge
- There are measurable and time based objectives
- There is a plan to show what is to be benchmarked
- Plan shows how and from where data will be collected
- Plan shows how and where "best practice" could be identified
- Plan shows how and where "best practice" could be identified
- Plan defines how to monitor the implementation of best practices
- Plan shows clear timescale for each step
- Plan predicts best and worst case results
- Plan defines a review of achievements.

22: The Five Ss

The Five Ss is a Japanese approach designed to focus attention on the basics of cleanliness and organisation. The phrase "Everything in its place and a place for everything", goes a long way to explaining the Five S system. The approach is founded on the principle that it is very difficult, if not impossible, to improve performance without order and cleanliness. The system focuses, therefore, on achieving effective workplace organisation, a clearly laid-out and well-defined work environment and achieves waste reductions while simultaneously improving quality and safety.

The Five Ss relate to five Japanese words:

- **Seiri – Sorting out:** Keep only those items in a work area that are necessary. If parts, components or tools are only needed occasionally, keep them in a storage area, not in the work area. If items are no longer needed, then recycle or dispose of them. Seiri tackles the habit of keeping things because they might be useful, someday. By reducing clutter, it is easier to find what is required. Also, valuable floor space can be released for additional production or new projects at minimal cost.

- **Seiton – Systematic arrangement:** The Shadow Board is a classic example of Seiton, the search for the most effective arrangement of tools and materials to have them available in the most efficient way. Mark the floor areas or storage areas to highlight where and how materials, finished goods and tools are to be stored and handled for maximum efficiency.

- **Seiso – Spic and span:** Clean the work place and keep it clean. Cleaning the workspace often leads to a safer working environment, as less clutter and clear passages make it easier and safer to complete work. Cleaning can also be seen as providing a basic level of inspection. If leaks, cracks, breakages or misalignments are detected early, then remedial action can take place before machines fail and production is lost.

- **Seiketsu – Standardising:** Set the new standard. Unless the new, clean and organised standard is defined, then human nature will ensure that he place reverts to the old ways. Involve people in setting and raising the standard further.

- **Shitsuke – Self discipline or Perseverance:** Keep with the standard, and ensure that people keep their areas at, or above, the defined standard. People will internalise the standard through perseverance, until it becomes the norm.

The 5 S system is very basic, but also quite powerful.

Remember, managers set the standard for a business. If a low standard is acceptable, then that is what is achieved. If a high standard is the target, then it too will be achieved.

23: Total Productive Maintenance

Total Productive Maintenance (TPM) is an approach to improving business performance that was developed by the Japan Institute of Plant Maintenance (www.jipm.or.jp) in the mid-1960s. It has been used effectively by a number of leading organisations in Japan and worldwide to achieve operational excellence.

TPM focuses attention on the practical aspects of a process – the productivity, efficiency, availability and quality effectiveness of machinery and processes.

The approach looks at the harder side of operations equipment and processes rather than the softer management side of business, generally addressed by Total Quality Control and Total Quality Management systems. It is highly structured, with the involvement of all people within the business. **Figure 88** shows the eight "pillars" of the approach:

FIGURE 88: TPM - 8 PILLARS

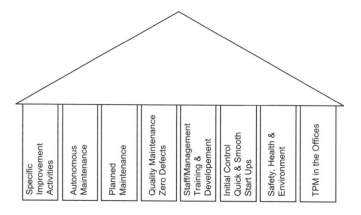

The focus of the approach is to achieve high reliability of processes and machinery, along with flexibility. Costs are reduced through the minimisation of wastage of man-hours, raw materials, machinery and consumables – in short, by achieving efficiencies and effectiveness in the traditional 3Ms of Man, Machinery and Materials.

The EU-Japan Centre for Industrial Co-operation (www.eu-japan.com) organised a series of study missions on best practice for European managers to Japan. Latterly, these missions have been called "TPM, the route to World Class Manufacturing".

The approach is useful as a means of capturing the embedded knowledge of a workforce through the widespread use of single page instruction sheets. Also, the focus on machine and process efficiencies can be very powerful.

However, the TPM approach is often a slow one, being quite demanding of manpower and resources to show real affects. Persistence is seen as a key characteristic of businesses using the TPM approach.

24: OVERALL EQUIPMENT EFFICIENCY

Overall Equipment Efficiency (OEE) is "the measure from Hell" – if one is a production manager. It is an extremely challenging way of measuring the overall capability and performance of an operation.

The measure is a composite of three factors to determine how effectively working hours are used. Overall Equipment Efficiency is defined as:

OEE = Availability X Performance Rate X Non-Defective Rate

Availability is a measure of the time lost due to downtime and it is calculated as:

Availability = (Loading Hours – Downtime) / Loading Hours

Loading Hours are defined as available working hours minus time allocated to production planning, time allocated for planned maintenance and planed daily management meetings.

Downtime is time lost due to unplanned activities such as breakdowns, adjustments or planned activities such as changeovers, set-ups or other occurrences.

The **Performance Rate** is another composite ratio. It is a combination of the Speed Operating Ratio and the Net Operating Ratio, defined by the Japan Institute of Plant Maintenance as:

Speed Operating Ratio = Reference Cycle Time / Actual Cycle Time

This ratio captures whether equipment and machinery are running at, beyond, or below design capability. It is defined as:

$$\text{Net Operating Ratio} = (\text{Actual Cycle Time X Number of Pieces Produced})/(\text{Loading Hours} - \text{Downtime})$$

This measure seeks to find out whether equipment is running consistently or erratically.

The **Non-Defective Rate** is calculated as:

$$\text{Non Defective Rate} = (\text{Total Number Processed - Number of Defective Units}))/\text{Total Number processed}$$

The number of defective units is first-time-pass units, any units that needed rework or re-generation should be counted as defective.

When these individual equations are brought together, we see that:

$$\text{OEE} = (\text{Standard Cycle Time X Number of Non-Defective Units})/\text{Loading Hours}$$

OEE is particularly suited to large volume production environments.

25: SIX SIGMA

The Six Sigma approach was developed by Motorola Corporation, as part of its efforts to achieve corporation-wide excellence. It is now used by Motorola as a key driver in its Continuous Improvement activity.

The approach builds upon the concepts of quality management tools and brings a high degree of rigour to their wide-spread application and use. The approach is used to focus a business on customer requirements, understanding processes within an operation and ensuring that they are aligned. It is centred on the rigorous use of analytical methods and requires appropriately timed intervention and action to address issues identified and for the implementation of responses and counter-measures.

The Six Sigma approach is centred around the reduction of variability within a process. As the focus is on customers' wants and needs, projects initiated under the Six Sigma approach start with the identification of a customer issue and end with the resolution of that issue. Effort is expended to make processes as near perfect as is humanly possible.

The Sigma refers to a statistical measure known as "standard deviation". By reducing the variability in a process, it is possible to reduce very significantly the opportunity for the process to be outside specification. If the process is not outside specification, then the customer gets what they want and require. In real terms, if a process is running at Six Sigma levels, then a fault or defect occurs no more than 3.4 times in every million parts.

Motorola also developed the DMAIC methodology to support the roll-out of the Six Sigma concept:

- **Define** the problem and the project to address it
- **Measure** and gather basic data as the starting point for the project
- **Analyse** the data, look for and identify root causes of defects
- **Improve** the process by addressing the key causes
- **Control** the process to ensure that it does not revert to the old ways.

The approach is highly disciplined and provides staff with the tools to manage and improve a process or product. It can be likened to using quality tools on steroids. Motorola regards it not purely as a quality methodology but rather as a way of doing business.

26: BUSINESS EXCELLENCE

The European Foundation for Quality Management provides businesses and organisations with a non-prescriptive framework to help them achieve true excellence (www.efqm.org). Because the model is non-prescriptive, it recognises the fact that there is no one best way to improve a process. Instead, it provides a number of basic concepts that are deemed to be fundamental to the achievement of excellence.

These fundamental concepts are, according to the EFQM:

- **Results Orientation:** A key driver for the organisation needs to be a focus on achieving results, results that exceed the expectations of all stakeholders and that, in fact, delight them.

- **Customer Focus:** Excellent organisations place significant emphasis on the achievement and delivery of sustainable customer value through a customer-focused orientation.

- **Leadership and Constancy of Purpose:** For an organisation to excel, it must have leadership of a high calibre – leadership that sees beyond the ordinary, that identifies and communicates a vision for the organisation that all can subscribe to. This vision needs to be coupled with resolve and constancy of purpose – it is not good enough to give in at the first signs of adversity. Leaders excel by creating and sharing a vision, and then leading an organisation to its achievement.

- **Management by Process and Facts:** Businesses are complex, it is important to understand the distinct processes and systems at work and to identify and develop coherent inter-relationships and effective management and improvement processes. The capturing of the facts of a business can lead to informed decisions being taken throughout an organisation, at the most appropriate level.

- **People Involvement and Development:** By involving and developing their people's capabilities and experience, businesses will maximise their contribution, flexibility and abilities.

- **Continuous Learning, Innovation and Improvement:** The market is constantly evolving and changing. To be competitive, an organisation needs to adopt the approach of Continuous Improvement, building on an ongoing basis its learning and innovation approaches and constantly seeking improvements.

- **Partnership Development:** Leading companies constantly look for value-adding partnerships in an effort to add value to their client interactions.

- **Corporate Social Responsibility:** The best organisations go beyond the basic minimum legal demands made of them. They seek to understand and develop their position within society and their contribution to it.

The Business Excellence Model developed by the EFQM consists of nine criteria, presented in **Figure 89**. These are broken down into five "Enablers" and four "Results". The enablers relate to what an organisation does, how it operates, its internal processes, while the results deal with what is achieved, the outputs. Detail of the model can be obtained from the web site (www.efqm.org).

FIGURE 89: EFQM BUSINESS EXCELLENCE MODEL

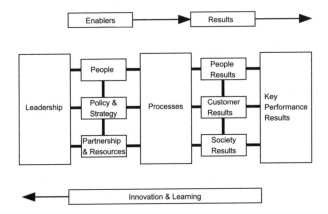

The original Business Excellence Model was heavily biased towards the needs and resources of large organisations. The EFQM continues to work to develop its SME-oriented model.

27: Value Management, Analysis & Engineering

The Value "family" covers a framework or approach that relies on a systematically-applied team-based approach to identifying and enhancing the value offered by a product or service.

The approach is function-oriented, seeking to understand where the costs and values of individual functions are located. By focusing on the cost/value equation in functional terms, an optimised balance of cost, performance and quality is achieved. The approach was pioneered by Lawrence D. Miles and much of his material is archived at University of Wisconsin-Madison (www.wisc.edu/wendt/miles/).

In general terms, Value Management (VM) is not a single method but an amalgam of methods brought together in a framework to achieve optimised value and function. The VM approach uses a closed feedback loop from the marketplace back to the designers, ensuring that experience gained from the marketplace is integrated into evolutionary and future design work.

The VM approach can be used on a project-by-project basis; however, companies that have championed the approach at senior management level have achieved major results by adopting a more strategic than project-based view.

The approach follows a systemised route now outlined.

The VM Steering Group

A steering group is formed with the objective of identifying the strategic areas of the business that will be tackled by VM. This group is often supported by an experienced, external VM facilitator. It is also normal that at least one member of the steering group has experience in using VM to act as a conduit to the other members of the group.

IDENTIFYING VM PRIORITIES

It is useful and important to identify key challenges facing the business, based on the strategic analysis of the steering group. As time and resources are limited, it is essential to prioritise key areas that are of high importance to the current and future success of the operation. These prioritised areas will provide direction when it comes to identifying specific VM projects.

IDENTIFYING VM PROJECTS

The prioritised challenge areas facing the business have been identified. It is now time to look for and choose projects that can have an impact on improving the business by reducing cost and increasing value.

It should be clear that choosing an achievable project is a good way to introduce VM to a business, rather than tackling a very large or difficult project first.

PERFORMING VM PROJECTS

The prioritised list of projects to be tackled has been developed, based on business needs.

Each project now requires a "Job Plan", consisting of:

1. **Planning:** Good planning usually leads to success. VM uses planning to:
   - Set the project objectives
   - Identify relevant team members
   - Capture the base information for the exercise
   - Discuss the project and consult with the staff
   - Plan a time line for specific actions
   - Identify whether there is a need for professional assistance

2. **Information Gathering:** The data relating to the project needs to be gathered to provide the project team with an objective starting point for their exercise.

3. **Analyse the data and project parameters/objectives:** One of the most powerful VM tools is that of Function Analysis – identifying what exactly a part, component, sub-system or system actually does. Since

a single item often performs a number of functions, it is essential to understand the functionality of all elements of a system before moving to change it. Flowcharting and process analysis tools are useful in assisting the mapping and understanding of processes.

4. **Creative Phase:** Enhancing the value. Techniques such as brainstorming are used in a structured way to challenge the team to identify potential improvements, radical changes, enhancements and cost savings for the project. Alternative methods, means and solutions are actively sought.

5. **Evaluating:** The body of ideas created in the previous phase need to be evaluated to identify which are most likely to succeed. The ideas are prioritised under three headings: cost or saving, time to implement and general practicality.

6. **Reporting:** Project teams report back to the Steering Group on their suggested solutions. These reports should be presented as business cases. Financial support material for suggested investments should accompany the reports, if appropriate.

7. **Implementing:** Proposals that have passed the reporting stage and accepted for implementation need to be acted upon.

8. **Follow-up Phase:** VM is focused on Value, by reducing costs, increasing functionality and meeting customer needs and requirements. It is very important to carry out follow-up, to ensure that the expected results of projects are realised.

The VM approach focuses the mind of all concerned on the true value of their products or services. The use of a structured approach helps ensure that the creative and innovative phases of an operation operate within the strategic plan of the business, with the objective of delivering real customer value.

28: LEAN PRODUCTION

Lean is about doing the most with the least: using less time, less stock, less people, less space and less money.

The Lean Production approach is as much a mind-set as a series of tools and techniques. Lean businesses use the tools of Physical and Process Flows, set-up time reduction, quality and people involvement throughout their full operations. The Lean Production approach is, in effect, the implementation of the Toyota Production System and follows the Japanese Kaizen or Continuous Improvement approach, whereby small incremental improvements are constantly sought. The Lean system also seeks to find step changes in production or operational performance, once again supported by Continuous Improvement after the step change has been made.

The system seeks to minimise inventory, by driving batch sizes towards the theoretical minimum of one. This approach puts the pressure on machine and process reliability and the achievement of quick change-over times and minimised set-up times. The system also puts pressure on processes to perform at high quality levels, as security stocks are kept at a minimum.

The system works to develop coherency along the value chain from supplier through operations, logistics and on to the customer and end-user. The latest systems also address the issues of end-of-life or lean recovery and recycling.

29: TARGET COST MANAGEMENT

Product creation and design is a risky business. It can be very demanding of manpower and cash, and a only small proportion of product concepts make it through to the marketplace.

Of all product failures, 40% are as a result of poor product planning, not understanding the market and its needs. A further 35% of product failures result from failure to fix the selling price of the product at the design concept stage. In total, 75% of new product failures are as a result of things that take place before true design work begins.

Most designers are focused on a product's performance or specification. Frequently, they are not concerned with either its cost or profitability, as they are often divorced from the realities of production or selling. This isolation can have a major impact on the profitability of products and the viability of a business. Almost all of the cost of a product is defined at the development and design phase of the product. The designers decide the key components and specifications of parts. Will gold be used, or silver, for the electrical contacts? Will the power plant be supplied by Mercedes or Skoda? Given the overwhelming effect of design decisions on the life costs of the product, it is clear that neither purchasing or manufacturing can make as big an impact on the overall cost of the product as the designers.

Target Cost Management (TCM) has evolved from basic costing systems and continuous improvement activities to help businesses contain product costs and ensure products meet both functional specifications and marketing and financial requirements. The approach provides a logical, scientific approach to product development.

TCM has five distinct steps:

- Planning
- Concept Design
- Basic Design
- Detailed Design
- Manufacturing Preparation.

Step1: Product Planning

A document is produced to capture key parameters, specifications and performance objectives for the new product. This document ensures that all elements of the business understand and agree with the outline parameters of the proposed new product.

The document typically includes:

1. Reason for the product to be developed with a description of the basic product concept – what it will do and how.

2. Basic specifications to define the performance envelope of the product. This section will usually include such items as a basic design time-line, including inputs and milestones from manufacturing and marketing.

3. The targeted cost point and the targeted selling price for the proposed product. The document will also include market projections, expected sales volumes, estimated profitability and estimated overall project development costs.

Step 2: Concept Design

Having outlined the proposed product, its target market and potential profitability for the business, it is necessary to decide whether the project is worth proceeding with. If the decision is to go forward, it is necessary to move towards Concept Design.

This phase usually consists of:

1. Definition of main functional elements of the product.

2. Distribution of key elements of cost to the top-level functional elements. What % of the targeted cost will be allocated to the engine, the body, the drive system, for example?

3. Initial outline designing of the key functional elements within the targeted costs.

4. Rough cost estimation to determine whether the original targeted cost appears to be achievable, and if not achievable, what steps will be taken to meet it?

5. Having completed the above four steps, the overall profitability of the product project is re-assessed and compared with the estimates prepared at Step 1: Product Planning.

If the project is still agreed to be viable and worthwhile, it moves on to the next step in the TCM process.

STEP 3: BASIC DESIGN

The process continues through the outline designing of sub-elements of the product, and leads to:

1. Distribution of costs not only to top level functions but to middle functions as well.
2. Creation of a general layout drawing of the proposed product under the targeted costs.
3. Determination of whether the product still meets the specifications, performance parameters and target costings using the current estimated costs.

STEP 4: DETAILED DESIGN

The product has successfully passed through the previous steps and is deemed to be suitable for taking on to the next stage of detailed design. At this time, detailed drawings are prepared for manufacturing purposes. This step usually includes:

1. Detailed drawings of design against the target costs to manufacturing detail level.
2. Carry out detailed cost estimation based on the detailed manufacturing drawings.

STEP 5: PREPARATION FOR MANUFACTURING

This stage deals with the details of manufacturing a product. Variations, options and model changes are planned for, as are necessary process developments. All these steps are undertaken within the constraint of the targeted cost. Designers, manufacturers and purchasing staff need to work closely together with the sales and marketing staff to find innovative and market acceptable ways to meet the targeted costs while increasing the overall value package of the products.

TCM is usually an iterative process. Designers need to be challenged to meet or exceed the targeted costs. There are two general methods of determining the manufacturing cost of a product, the Subtraction Method or the Addition Method.

- **Subtraction Method:** Where Manufacturing Cost Target = Selling Price – Gross Margin
- **Addition Method:** Where Selling Price = Manufacturing Cost + Profit.

The Subtraction Method is the method most in use in Japan, although it is clearly the more demanding choice.

CONCLUSION

We have now looked at the basic Level 1, 2 and 3 tools and techniques being used by leading organisations around the world to achieve improved performance. The upward route from Level 1, through Level 2 to Level 3 should be clear. We now go on to look at the broader context of improvement activities, how they can affect and influence national capability and ongoing competitiveness.

30: THE BIG PICTURE

The tools, techniques and concepts and approaches presented in this book have been developed and proven with small and medium-sized businesses located in Ireland over the past 10 years. Much of the work has been supported by academic research.

The focus so far has been on what can be done within individual businesses, to improve performance. This last chapter will provide some of the background context of this research work and its findings. It will also identify challenges facing a small, open economy if it is to achieve sustainable competitiveness into the future.

HOW IRELAND MEASURES UP

In the late 1990s, Ireland became known as the European "tiger" economy – The Celtic Tiger. In the late 1990s, we experienced very high levels of growth while maintaining low levels of inflation, a feat that still baffles many economists.

In the early 2000s, our level of inflation increased to 3% or 4%, but our growth rate was still the highest in the European Community, if not the developed world, and ran at nearly twice the European average. Our growth levels are presented in **Figure 90**.

FIGURE 90: THE GROWTH OF THE IRISH
ECONOMY

	GDP %	GNP %
1997	10.8	9.4
1998	8.6	7.9
1999	10.8	8.2
2000	11.5	10.4
2001	4.7	5.5
2002(e)	3.25	3.75

Ireland is a young nation still coming to terms with its independence. In the late 1950s, we were faced with massiv migr ion and very poor living standards. In the late 1970s and early 1980s, we were once again facing national meltdown. At the time, the standing joke was "would the last person to leave the island, please turn off the lights!". There was a general air of depression and gloom. Unemployment was at 18% and the level of National debt was at over 130% of GDP.

Today, Ireland is a changed place. Although we have been experiencing severe growing pains, with rising inflation and severe infrastructural problems, our growth rate is forecast to be the highest in the developed world at 3.5% and our Debt-to-GDP ratio was 36% in 2001 and is forecast to reach 34% in 2002. We are now facing problems of growth and expansion. All this while still being at the mercy of a volatile world economy. New problems for us.

LET'S LOOK AT THE FULL PICTURE!

The Tiger Economy was real but not all pervasive. While some businesses and citizens prospered, others found matters not quite so prosperous. We have a small open economy. We need to export to survive. *Per capita*, Ireland is the biggest exporter in the world. With the introduction of the Euro in January 2002, price levels across the European Community are much more transparent than before. This is putting severe pressure on Irish suppliers to meet and exceed the competitiveness levels of our European partners. If we look at the competitiveness of Irish industry, we see some strange anomalies (**Figure 91**).

FIGURE 91: IRISH COMPETITIVENESS RANKING

COUNTRY	Company Size (# employees)		
	0-5	10-49	50-250
Ireland	15th	15th	2nd
Germany	3rd	3rd	3rd

Source: National Competitiveness Council, Annual Report.

Looking the figures in more detail, we can see how Ireland ranks against the rest of our European partners, in **Figure 92**.

FIGURE 92: IRISH PRODUCTIVITY RANKING WITHIN EUROPE

COUNTRY	Company Size (# employees)		
	0-9	10-49	50-249
Austria	17	12	4
Belgium	1	2	6
Denmark	10	9	12
Finland	13	16	16
France	6	9	11
Germany	3	3	3
Greece	16	17	18
Iceland	7	12	9
Ireland	*15*	*15*	*2*
Italy	4	4	5
Luxembourg	7	1	1
Netherlands	7	5	14
Norway	13	5	10
Portugal	18	18	17
Spain	5	9	12
Sweden	12	5	14
Switzerland	2	12	8
UK	10	5	7

Source: National Competitiveness Council, Annual Report.

It is clear that our small to medium-sized companies have a competitiveness problem. We need to focus resources on helping them resolve this issue. Specific focus needs to be given to the needs, issues and resources of SMEs to tackle the problem.

Small to medium-sized companies are very important to the strength of an economy. European research has shown that SMEs generate over 70% of turnover in the European Community and account for between 65% - 85% of value-added. Almost 70% of all employed people in Europe are employed in small and medium-sized businesses.

In Ireland, we have about 5,000 companies involved in industrial production (CSO). The breakdown of companies by size is presented in **Figure 93**.

FIGURE 93: IRISH INDUSTRIAL COMPANIES BY SIZE

Employee Numbers	1-9	10-49	50-99	100-199	200-249	250-500
No. of Companies	1,901	2,276	477	325	53	118

Looking at data for leading industrial nations, we see a different picture regarding company size, as shown in **Figure 94**.

FIGURE 94: INDUSTRIAL COMPANIES BY SIZE IN OTHER COUNTRIES

COUNTRY	Percentage of companies in employee number bands				
	1-9	10-19	20-99	100-499	500 +
USA	12	8	18	14	47
UK	26	6	16	17	34
Germany	21	10	18	18	33
Ireland	36	21	31	9	1

It is clear that Ireland has a larger proportion of smaller companies. If the Irish economy is to be sustainable into the future, these small and medium-sized companies need to build their capabilities, effectiveness and efficiency.

PRACTICE LINKED TO PERFORMANCE

It seems very obvious to say that if you do the right thing (Practice), you will achieve the right result (Performance). In the late 1990s, academic research finally proved this linkage for business. A positive link was found between the practices businesses employed and the level of performance that they achieved. This is a significant find for business. We can now be assured that, if we invest time and effort in adopting best practice, we will get a business reward.

Research work by Prof. Chris Voss of the London Business School (1994) examined the benchmark results from hundreds of European companies and developed a classification system with six levels:

- **Group A** : World Class - Staying in Front
- **Group B** : Contenders - En Route
- **Group C** : Promising – Inhibited
- **Group D** : Inefficient – Seeming to get "Something for Nothing"
- **Group E** : Vulnerable - Where to Start?
- **Group F** : At Risk.

Details of what each classification grouping means and the challenges facing businesses in each grouping are presented in **Appendix II**.

In 2000, an Irish study compared 180 Irish SMEs against the results of thousands of European SMEs. The results of this study were published as the "Made in Ireland" report (Enterprise Ireland). **Figure 95** looks at the results of this report and compares them with European data. Figure 100 also presents the percentage of companies in each of the five Microscope classifications in each of the relevant geographical areas.

FIGURE 95: PERCENTAGE OF COMPANIES IN EACH MICROSCOPE CLASSIFICATION

	UK	Belgium	Italy	Rest of Europe	Ireland
At Risk	1	7	39	0	4
Vulnerable	18	6	8	14	27
Inefficient	37	26	31	31	23
Contenders	39	49	2	48	39
World Class	0	0	0	4	1

Source: Made in Ireland Report, Enterprise Ireland.

An analysis of the figures shows that Ireland has a large tail of companies in the lower regions, with a significant number either At Risk or Vulnerable. This long tail of poor performers seems to explain why Ireland ranks 15th in terms of European productivity. If we are to address this situation, it is important that Irish SMEs move to adopt best practice.

CONCLUSION

This book has tried to present a picture of the challenges facing Irish business, as well as a picture of some possible answers to the many issues facing today's managers. The use of objective benchmarking provides people with clear indications of how good they are and also where they need to focus their improvement efforts.

The basic World Class Business tools outline key practices that have proven helpful to many Irish businesses in their efforts to improve. The tools have worked well in very many sectors, in very many different sized businesses, in every corner of the island.

The three levels of implementation have presented a step-by-step guide to the effective use of these tools.

The challenge now facing Irish business is: **Are we mature enough to take on the task of really competing with the best?**

If we are committed to operating at even higher levels of performance, then we are almost assured of success. We are intelligent, well-educated, creative people who can and do work hard. The future of our country and our children rests with us. Are we up to the challenge?

Appendix I: Self Assessment Questionnaire

Introscope is a simple benchmarking tool, designed to introduce people working in a wide variety of businesses and organisations to the power of benchmarking.

Using a sample of questions drawn from some of the best available benchmarking tools, Introscope invites you (perhaps with a few colleagues) to assess some of your organisation's key practices and performance aspects against a model of "best practice", and to discover how your assessments compare to those of hundreds of other organisations. Start by confirming the scope of your assessment, which could be a department, site or the whole organisation – it will work at any of these levels, so long as you are consistent.

If you find Introscope and its outputs useful, ask about the range of more sophisticated benchmarking tools from which you can select one suitable for your needs. You will have to invest a little more effort, but you are likely to find this well worthwhile as benchmarking results help you to shape your improvement plans with confidence.

How to Score

You choose the statement most appropriate to your organisation/site and this gives you a score – the number in the grey band above, 1,3, or 5. Sometimes, you may feel that your organisation is between two statements. In this case you choose the number between the two statements, 2 or 4.

If you see differences across the organisation, where some areas are more advanced than others, it is best to assess an average position. For example, a pilot implementation does not warrant the maximum score of five. We seek to assess the your position TODAY, not where it will be when current plans and projects deliver the results you expect. Benchmarking will only ever be of value to you if assessments are true reflections of the practices and performance of the organisation as it is NOW.

The INTROScope questions

INTROScope questions are drawn from the longer questionnaire scripts used by five of the best available benchmarking tools:

- Manufacturing Microscope
- Service Microscope
- The Micro Business Review
- Manufacturing PROBE

- Service PROBE.

		1	3	5
1	**Role of leadership in developing customer-focused culture**	Little attention paid by top management	Supported by top management, delegated down	Top management visibly promotes and actively participates
2	**Service/product meeting customer needs**	Service/product does not consistently meet the customer needs	Service/product generally meets customer needs	Service/product produces results that consistently meet and exceed customer needs
3	**Quality performance, relative to industry**	Poor overall quality record, compared to industry	Achieved levels about equal to the industry standard	Achieved a reputation for excellence in quality services and products that is notable in the industry and significantly better than the competition
4	**The time it takes**	We lose some business because it takes longer than customers want to wait to make/ deliver our products/services	Our speed is neither a strength nor a weakness for us in gaining business	We win business because we are quicker than the competition
5	**Quality mind-set**	Problems will happen. Deal with customer complaints.	Inspection and control with some data collection.	Total quality mindset. Quality is everyone's job, and employees take ownership of process.
6	**Training and education**	Ad hoc, no plan	Some skills and development training for all employees	More than 5% of each employee's time devoted to training with strong emphasis on quality
7	**Problem-solving**	Crisis mindset, confusion, finger-pointing	System for recognizing and responding to problems, emphasis on process not people, teamwork	Problems viewed as opportunities for further improvement, employees empowered to correct
8	**Employee morale**	Pressure and stress, anxiety about future, cynicism	Stability, *status quo* or moderate progress, occasional stress situations	Controlled environment, growth opportunities, consensus on direction, optimism and confidence.

		1	3	5
9	**Innovativeness**	No recent innovations in service/product concept and process	Regular innovations in service/product and an occasional major breakthrough innovation	Many innovations; recognised as a leading innovator in industry/segment
10	**New service/product design and development process**	No identifiable process for improving existing services/products or for new service development	Ad hoc basis; services/products developed and improved regularly but no set process	Formal and reproducible process for developing new and enhancing existing services/products
11	**Management of business processes**	No attention to business processes (for example, customer billing process)	Key processes defined and mapped; initial steps taken toward redesigning and improving these processes	Key business processes managed and redesigned where needed; process owners in place; process performance measured
12	**Reliability of equipment and machinery**	We only maintain things when they break down. Perhaps this is why we have frequent problems with equipment (computers; equipment used in delivery of our products/services)	Maintenance is carried out to the maker's instructions. We plan time for this in order to reduce the risk of failure. We have adequate data security and back-up procedures	We take maintenance seriously. We try to anticipate problems and are prepared to invest time/money to prevent them. The people who use the equipment day to day take responsibility for looking after it.
13	**Housekeeping**	Cluttered and disruptive	Organised	Clean, orderly, minimum work-in-progress, self-maintained, always 'tour ready'.
14	**Relationships with Suppliers**	Many vendors, seek low bid, no certification programme	A few certified suppliers, Just-in-Time for hardware and consumables	Partnerships with certified suppliers, Just-in-Time deliveries, involved in product/service and process design improvements
15	**Product/ Operating costs**	Product/Operating costs greater than the competition	Competitive	Product/ Operating costs lowest in the industry
16	**Level of customer satisfaction**	Customer expectation often not met; some customer complaints	Little customer dissatisfaction; expectations met, but rarely exceeded	Many delighted customers; customers will enthusiastically recommend the service/product to others; expectations often exceeded

		1	3	5
17	**Customer Satisfaction measurement**	Limited measurement of customer satisfaction	Regular measurement of customer satisfaction in large, broad-based samples of customers	Careful identification of the dimensions of customer satisfaction by segment, using a broad range of measurement tools
18	**Performance measurement and reporting**	By costs and sales volumes (accounting/finance-driven)	By costs and non-financial measures of process outcomes	Using multiple measures (a balanced scorecard such as customer satisfaction, market share, employee morale and financial)

Organisation's name:
Unit or Site name:
Type of Organisation:
Number of people working in the organisation:
Address (full postal):
Post code:
Telephone (and code):
Fax (and code):
e-mail address:
Name and position of person responding:
Date:
Name of adviser & organisation:

All information in this questionnaire is confidential.
Your answers will be used by your advisor/advisory organisation to give you confidential feedback, which should help you to develop an action plan. The information about your organisation's practices/performance will also be used as an anonymous contribution to future benchmarking analysis.

© University of Northumbria at Newcastle 2001

Introscope has been developed by the Centre for Business Excellence at Northumbria University with support from the PROBE partnership, and is managed on their behalf by Comparison International.
www.cbe.unn.ac.uk www.comparisoninternational.com

Appendix II: Facilitated Assessment & Comparison Tools

In **Chapter 2**, we considered Faciliatated Assessment Benchmarking (FAB). In Europe today, two leading FAB tools exist:

- **Microscope / Probe** – a largely qualitative approach, focusing mainly on the practices and systems businesses use: www.comparisoninternational.com

- **BenchmarkIndex** – a largely quantitative system, focused on capturing the hard measures of performance being achieved: www.benchmarkindex.com.

These tools have many thousands of benchmark data sets captured from businesses in Europe and beyond, in America, Australia and the Far East.

Microscope / Probe Classification System

The work of Professor Chris Voss and others resulted in the generation of a six-level classification system for companies dependent on their benchmark results. This system is now presented, along with the challenges facing a company if they are located in each classification.

- **Group A : World Class - Staying in Front:** This group is representative of leading companies, they need to focus on building global capability, achieving rapid time to market, exploiting know-how of all partners, achieving a step change in costs. They also need to focus on providing their customers with mass customisation and be able to achieve environmental differentiation. In short they need to focus on new ways to delight their customers.

- **Group B : Contenders - En Route:** These companies have many of the characteristics of the leading companies and are well placed to reach full world class status, they need to aim for "delighted" customers, to strive to achieve market driven quality. To work to improve their operations using the EFQM/Baldridge templates. They need to focus on getting employee involvement and building an ethos of social and environmental responsibility. In short, they need to focus on service excellence.

- **Group C : Promising – Inhibited:** This group has a number of definite problems to overcome, quite often typified by poor management buy-in and commitment to continuous improvement. They have to build executive commitment, develop a flat organisation, and move to achieving employee empowerment, building their skills and developing effective training. They need to focus on building teamwork between their staff. They should be using benchmarking and introducing measurement and incentives to help guide them to improved performance.

- **Group D : Inefficient – Seeming to get "Something for Nothing":** This group would appear to be getting "something for nothing", they tend to be working harder than necessary to deliver the levels of performance they are achieving. An example of this could be in terms of delivered quality. They exhibit high delivered product quality, often without the benefit of a quality system, but quite often at the expense of full product final inspection rather than through the use of high quality processes. This high level of final inspection adds unnecessary cost to the product and ht operation. They need to focus on developing a quality vision, building their customer and supplier partnerships. They need to tackle the problems of eliminating unnecessary cost from their operations and move towards a feeling of business process ownership among their staff. They need to focus on achieving effectiveness and efficiency.

- **Group E : Vulnerable - Where to Start?:** Probably the companies with the biggest problems, they are faced with the issue of recognising there is a crisis. They suffer from poor executive vision and lack a customer satisfaction focus. They tend to have little or no employee involvement and have major opportunities for process improvement. They need to focus on introducing control and predictability into their operations.

- **Group F : At Risk:** These companies are faced with the question of survival before attempting to improve.

APPENDIX III: SOURCES OF FURTHER INFORMATION

Browne, Steve (1996). Strategic Manufacturing for Competitive Advantage, *Transforming operations from shop floor to strategy*, Prentice Hall,

Hayes, R. & Pisano, G. (1994). Beyond World Class: The New Manufacturing Strategy, *Harvard Business Review*, January-February, pp. 77-86.

Kanter, R. (1991). Managing Change in Innovative Organizations in *The Quest for Competitiveness*, Shetty, Y. & Buehler, V. (eds), Quorum, New York.

Kenney, M. & Florida, R. (1993). *Beyond Mass Production*, Oxford University Press, New York.

Made in Ireland Report, Enterprise Ireland, 2001.

mu.motorola.com/ : Six Sigma information.

National Competitiveness Council (2000). *Annual Competitiveness Report 2000*, Forfás, Dublin.

Peters, T. & Waterman, R., (1982). *In Search of Excellence*, Harper & Row, New York.

Pierre Fortin (2000). *The Irish Economic Boom: Facts, Causes and Lessons*, Paper prepared for Industry Canada.

www.benchmarkindex.com : Benchmark Index.

www.benchmarking-in-europe.com : European Benchmarking Information.

www.comparisoninternational.com : Microscope Benchmark.

www.dti.gov.uk/mbp/ : Management Best Practice site of Department Trade and Industry, UK.

www.efqm.org : European Foundation for Quality Management.

www.enterprise-ireland.com : Support for developing indigenous industry.

www.eujapan.com : EU Japan Centre for Industrial Co-operation.

www.excellence-ireland.ie : Excellence Ireland, Irish focal point for business excellence, quality and hygiene marks.

www.irishbenchmarkingforum.com : Irish Benchmarking information.

www.jipm.or.jp : Japanese Institute for Plant Maintenance.

www.onbusiness.ie/ndm

www.wisc.edu/wendt/miles/ : Value Engineering resource

INDEX

OAK TREE PRESS

Ireland's leading business book publisher,
Oak Tree Press is increasingly an international
developer and publisher of small business training
and support solutions.

Oak Tree Press has developed "platforms" of
Pre-start-up, Start-up, Growth and Support content,
which include books and workbooks, websites,
software, assessment models, training, consultancy
and certification.

Oak Tree Press' small business training and support
solutions are in use in Ireland, the UK, USA,
Scandinavia and Eastern Europe and are available for
customisation to local situations and needs.

For further information, contact:
Brian O'Kane

OAK TREE PRESS

19 Rutland Street, Cork, Ireland
T: + 353 21 431 3855   F: + 353 21 431 3496
E: info@oaktreepress.com
W: www.oaktreepress.com

www.oaktreepress.com